A Dream Come True
A Rugby League Life

Doug Laughton
with Andrew Quirke

LONDON LEAGUE PUBLICATIONS LTD

A Dream Come True
A Rugby League Life

A CIP catalogue record for this book is available from the British Library.

First published in Great Britain in October 2003 by:
London League Publications Ltd, P.O. Box 10441, London E14 0SB

ISBN: 1-903659-12-4

Cover design by: Stephen McCarthy Graphic Design
                                    46, Clarence Road, London N15 5BB

Layout: Peter Lush

Printed and bound by: Biddles Ltd, Guildford and Kings Lynn

Foreword

That Doug Laughton was destined to become an international Rugby League player was never in doubt, such was the commitment, the enthusiasm, and the confidence he displayed as a youngster alongside me in the pack at St Helens in the Sixties. That he should become one of the game's most successful coaches with Widnes and Leeds was understandable given his application to, and his passion for, the XIII-a-side code. But that he was a media man's dream, a larger than life personality, and one who strove to take the game, both on and off the pitch, far beyond its traditional boundaries owed much to the character and charisma of the man himself.

Doug enjoyed his rugby and he made sure that everyone else enjoyed it with him. Whether tucked away at the side of the showers in a cramped Widnes dressing room at Naughton Park or squeezed into his office in the 'corridor of power' at Headingley, Doug welcomed all with news of his latest signings and revealed his 'exclusives' to those who cared to celebrate a good result with him. His sense of humour, his warmth to anyone who, like him, respected and supported his game, and his friendly, open nature enabled him to handle the players, the directors, and the media with style. And that style was reflected on the field when his daring raids on the world of Rugby Union enabled him to link up the likes of Martin Offiah, Alan Tait, Craig Innes, Jim Fallon, John Devereux, Paul Moriarty, Emosi Koloto, Jonathan Davies and others with the best local talent around.

Doug Laughton's teams played as he did, with flair, with vision, and with a certain panache. He served the sport for over 40 years as a player and a coach while his attitude and sense of humour during that period helped us to realise that what he played and coached was only a game. The friendships forged in rugby and the apocryphal stories recalled are more lasting than our remembrance of the results themselves. And I'm sure readers will recall the many dramatic and amusing episodes contained in Doug's autobiography long after they have forgotten the result of a particular match. That's how I remember Doug Laughton, and I'm sure that, when you have read his fascinating account of his life in Rugby League, you will too.

Ray French

Ray French played at St Helens with Doug Laughton. He also played for Widnes and Great Britain. Since retiring from playing, he has become one of the sport's most distinguished writers, and is also BBC Television's chief Rugby League commentator.

Andrew Quirke

Andrew Quirke is a St Helens RLFC supporter, who along with fellow fan Kevin Gill wrote the Saints fanzines *Saints To Win* and *Rart Up T' Tash* before the pair moved onto the independent St Helens RLFC website *Ruttweb*. Andrew's first book *Knowsley Road - Memories of St Helens Rugby League Football Club* was published in September 2001 by London League Publications Ltd.

Andrew can testify first-hand how good Doug Laughton's cooking is and alongside seeing family and friends and following Saints, it is one of the few things he misses about life in Britain as he is currently (September 2003) lucky enough to be living in Sydney, Australia for a year. He has adopted Sydney Roosters as his NRL team and can often be found watching them with a pie and sauce plus schooners at Aussie Stadium.

Thank You

Doug Laughton, Andrew Quirke and London League Publications Ltd would like to thank the following people for their help and support in producing this book:
Chris Anderson, Eric Ashton, Dave Bettley, Reg Bowden, Kel Coslett, Mike Critchley, Francis Cummins, Phil Daly, Ray French, John Huxley, Steve Kilgallon Alex Murphy and Frank Myler for their contributions and support.
Dave Farrar for proof-reading.
Raymond Fletcher for providing the statistics.
Michael O'Hare for subediting work.
Steve McCarthy for design work on the cover.
All the photographers who provided photographs.

Bibliography

Widnes Weekly News
Rugby Rebel - The Alan Tait Story by Alan Tait with Bill Lothian (Mainstream - 1998)
Offiah My Autobiography by Martin Offiah with David Lawrenson (Collins Willow - 1997)
Code Breaker by Jonathan Davies with Peter Corrigan (Bloomsbury - 1996)
Widnes RLFC Hall of Fame Brochure by Sam Patmore, Ron Girvin, Stephen Fox, John Potter & Chris Moore.
The Rugby League Challenge Cup – An Illustrated History by Les Hoole (Breedon Books 1998)
Widnes Rugby League Football Club – A Pictorial History by Leslie Woodhead (Archive Publications 1989)

Contents

Note: Match reports and introductions to chapters 7 and 15 in italics were
written by Peter Lush.

1. Was there a factory for making canes?

I was born in May 1944, and grew up in one of a row of terraced houses, an area of Widnes that seemed to be just a conveyor belt for producing factory workers.

When I was six, we moved to Steward's Avenue, a horseshoe-shaped road. There we had a bathroom, garden and inside toilet which we didn't have before. Before we moved, I went to St Marie's Infants school and then, when we moved, to St Bede's Primary School. I played some Rugby League there, but at school my best sport was swimming. It doesn't mix with Rugby League, because swimming makes your muscles soft.

At the bottom of Steward's Avenue was Hood Road, and living there was the legendary Great Britain loose-forward Vinty 'The Wild Bull of the Pampas' Karalius. And a stone's throw away from my back garden lived Widnes Rugby League legend Frank Myler. The two of them were heroes of mine, but Vinty was my idol.

My dream when I was growing up was to be Vinty. I remember telling people that I had matched strides with Vinty. As he walked along the road, I would walk with him, trying to match his stride. I wanted to do what he had done; I remember thinking that I wanted to lift the cup at Wembley just like Vinty. And he would always speak to us kids. When I walked alongside him, he would ask what I was up to and I would tell him that I was matching strides with him and that 'I am going to be a good player like you'. He would just say that would be good, and pat me on the head.

My first real impressions of Rugby League came in our terraced house; all sitting round listening to the big wireless. You couldn't always afford to go to the big games in those days.

But my mam did take me sometimes, and I remember my dad taking me to see Saints playing Barrow in the 1956 Challenge Cup semi-final replay at Wigan. The ground was unbelievably packed – there were 44,731 there - and my dad had to put me on his shoulders so I could see the game. I thought it was tremendous. I remember watching Steve Llewellyn scoring a try after starting from behind his own line. He went the full length of the field to score and I sat on my dad's shoulders thinking: 'One day I'll do that'. I never did, mind you.

I also remember when I was about nine or 10, my mam taking me to a cup match at Workington. In those days, the game was played under the unlimited tackle rule, which meant one team kicked-off and the opposition seemed to keep the ball up their jumpers until half time, and then hoping that, after the interval, the first team would lose the ball from the kick off.

1

Unfortunately Widnes dropped the ball, and the culprit took a high swing at an opponent. This gave Workington a penalty which they kicked and they kept the ball for the rest of the game so we were out of the cup. I thought at the time, even though I was a nine-year-old, that the unlimited tackle rule needed changing.

Jerry Laughton, my great uncle, played stand-off and Paddy Douglas, my great granddad, scrum-half for Widnes in the 1930 Challenge Cup Final victory over odds-on favourites St Helens. Laughton was my dad's surname and Douglas was my mam's surname: it was definitely a Rugby League family, which is how the game spread in those days.

I actually supported Widnes when I was growing up, but I liked to watch St Helens' Alex Murphy. In 1961, Widnes drew 5-5 at St Helens in the Challenge Cup first round and coming out of the ground all you could hear the St Helens supporters saying was: 'Murphy's not played'. I was thinking: 'How good is this Murphy?' I soon found out - he scored three tries in the replay as Saints won 29-10 and went on to win the cup. That was the first time I saw him play. He is the greatest player I have ever seen in my life.

Murphy could read your mind on and off the field, he saved my career and he made me a better player. While Vinty Karalius was my idol and the player I wanted to be like, I was, like Murphy, a scrum-half at secondary school. Although I wasn't big enough to play in the pack but I still had dreams of playing loose-forward. I always think if you set your goals high, you'll make it, and my goal was to be another Vinty Karalius.

When I was young, you had to be a rebel to get fed. If you were lucky enough to have a chicken in your house for tea, the news would spread like wildfire.

'He's got a chicken'.

'He's got a chicken?'

'He has you know, he has got a chicken'.

'Has your dad had a good win? Has he got a yank up on the horses?'

I would be swaggering down the street with my chest out proudly saying: 'We've got a chicken' and I don't see anything wrong with that. People don't realise how hard it was. Now a chicken means nothing, in those days it was big news. I would just be praying that I got more than two slices off the chicken. If your mam got three doubles and a treble you might even get a leg of lamb. If you did, you knew you weren't to ask for any more when it was dished up as you would get a crack and a reminder that the rest was for dad's butties. I remember going to the corner shop and not be able to afford anything. Now you can go to ASDA for some milk and a loaf of bread and end up coming back with a full trolley, but people don't seem as happy as they were in those days. As a kid I remember being fed dripping butties and even worse, sugar butties. How bad were they? That's all you had.

As for Christmas, I would have a little stocking which contained an orange, a tangerine and a little plastic crab. Chocolate was rare, but if your dad got another yank up you might get a bike as the years went on. It was so poor back then though and people forget. Three in a bed in those days meant you and your two brothers having to share a single bed. And some fellow used to go round waking people up by knocking on their windows with a big stick, as we didn't have alarm clocks. I was terrified by that - I was only six. I was thinking that maybe the hard upbringing makes you a better player, but then realised that the Australians do it now without all that. Some people say it's down to them having a nice climate, I just think they do things well.

My older sister Jean says I was a proper whinger as a toddler, which isn't surprising really. You were strapped into a go chair in those days, with solid tyres and no spring - in fact, a torture machine. There's little Douglas, two and a half years old, strapped in and pushed miles over cobbled streets yelling. I think that's where the saying 'shake the living daylights out of him' came from.

An average day for me was something like this. My dad would come home from work and my mam would say: 'Give him the belt; he's been a little sod all day'. I probably had. I just thought: 'Here we go again' and I got the belt. My mam would be doing the washing at the tub and when you've got a lot of kids it must be hard, but she'd still give me a crack. People used to say: 'Look at the bumps on your head, that's your brain bursting with knowledge' and I used to say 'It's nothing to do with knowledge, it's where me mam's belted me'.

If you got caught cheating or lying, you were in big trouble. I used to come in late from school and my mam would ask me where I had been and I would tell her that I had been the library getting some books. What had really happened is that I had been kissing behind the bushes after school and had then sprinted to the library and grabbed the first books I could. 'You lying little so and so', she replied, and crack, that was it.

When I was 14 years old, I remember tying the town clerk up in knots. I spoke to him about some houses that were being built and that I felt he had got his sums wrong. I was good at maths, but he said: 'I'm the town clerk, I'm not wrong'. Now when I know I'm right, I'm like a rat on a kipper. I was telling him about interest rates and so on and had him 'pots for rags' even though I was only 14. I later got a letter from him that I wish I'd kept, saying that I had a promising future and that it was a shame

I was going to be a painter and decorator for the Corporation. The first thing I was taught in maths is that if you can divide and multiply by 10 and move the decimal point, it'll get you everywhere.

I always wanted to win at whatever I did. No one could beat me in the swimming baths; I was a good swimmer. I was also a good slip fielder at cricket - if it went in the slips, it would stick there. But I batted like a poor man's Geoffrey Boycott. Nobody could get me out, but I'd seldom knock a run. I wasn't a bad bowler, mind you. There was one kid who used to play called Bentley and he was a great cricketer. I thought later 'What happened to him?' He had a great talent, but just didn't seem that bothered. I didn't think I had any great talent for cricket. I never thought that and still don't to this day. I didn't want to have a go at anything unless I could win, what was the point of playing if you couldn't win?

Later, when I embarked upon my professional Rugby League playing career, I was the worst loser in the world: I used to sulk for days if we lost. If we lost the last game of the season I would sulk all the close season. I hated it, I just couldn't cope with it and it didn't matter if we lost a league game or a cup final, every game was the same. My wife used to say: 'Let our lad win when he plays you at draughts'. I said let him get his own wins. When he did beat me, I thought: 'Right, we'll move onto chess'. When he beat me at chess, I thought 'I don't want to play any more games with you'. If I can't win, I don't want to play. The only thing that makes it bearable is that you can accept defeat because you know you've got another chance next week. The moment you're happy being a loser that's all you'll ever be. You can't change history but you still have to go through the pain of losing, even though I found it devastating.

I went to Fisher Moore Secondary, which should have been called Fisher Moore Six of the Best. I thought it was another conveyor belt for factory workers. If you smiled in class there, you got six of the best, it was unbelievable. I'm sure they had a hand at home that they used to practice on. I would say 'Three on that hand, sir and then three on this one, I hope you got pleasure out of that sir'. I was a rebel, and they made me pain-free, because it got to the stage where I realised it didn't hurt me anymore. I hated authority, which would later cause me to fall out with Saints and Wigan during my playing career. I was the upstart. I was told at school: 'Get out of here, what are you smiling for?' I like to smile; I don't see what harm it causes. They said it was a smirk. I would describe it as a wry smile. I've always seen things that other people don't see, and things that amuse me don't always amuse other people. I suppose I've got a warped

Off to Wembley: An outing as a youngster to support Widnes

sense of humour. I know I could be awkward and too smart for my own good at times.

I remember I fell asleep once during a science class and I got whacked around the head with a cane. I'd fallen asleep because the teacher was boring the pants off me. I never sleep in the day and I've never done it since, that's the only time I've slept during the day, so he must have been painfully dull. He had a droning, monotonous voice too, the type of person whom if I talked to now, I'd be looking for the fire escape.

I took exception to being hit, I don't like being hit, never have done and never will. If you hit me, I'll hit you back, only hopefully twice as hard. I was only five foot four inches and this teacher was six foot six and he was hitting me with a stick. If they'd have given me a sword, I'd have fought the swine. That's the kid I was. All these people who behaved towards you like that and made life hard for you are the same people that, when you become a star in the game, want to know you. That annoyed me even more. They made me a prefect and later house captain while I was there, basically because they couldn't control me.

I remember a teacher keeping me in once and telling me I had to write 500 lines. Earlier, he'd put a crossword up on the blackboard, it must have taken him days to do it. One clue asked 'what rattles in the cupboard?' Well, we had this kid in the class called Kilgannon, so while the teacher was out of the room, I wrote Kilgannon as my answer on the board. Everyone else in the class was shouting things out. The teacher came in, asked who had done it and told us we were all staying behind. Nobody owned up, so I put my hand up. He told me I would have to stay behind. I didn't think it fair as I had done one, but wasn't the only one who had been writing things on the board.

So I'm sitting there and I've got to write these 500 lines, so I put these three pens together and start writing: 'I must not write on the blackboard'. The teacher asked me what I was doing; I told him I was writing my lines. He said 'One pen'. I thought: 'Well, I've had it now'. So I started writing really slowly and he asked me what I was doing. I said: 'Well, to be honest sir, I was writing them quickly because I've got to get the spuds from the shop, peel the spuds for tea and light the fire for when me mam gets home from work. I can't do that now, so I'm going to get the belt whatever I do - so we might as well stay together, I like you.'

'Bugger off home', he said, 'and get the spuds peeled'. In other words, he didn't want to stay until 7pm with me. You learn your lessons in life - everyone can be worked.

I remember at secondary school being told to run the 440 yards. As I was lining up, there was a lad in our class who we called 'the skeleton' alongside me. I thought: 'Well at least I'll beat him'. He did me on the line, I was 13-and-a-half, beaten in the 440 but I could catch wingers, so I thought: 'I've had enough of this' and turned to Rugby League.

I've always been a competitor, but I had thought Rugby League was too hard for me. And that was to happen again in my life - a lot of times I nearly quit the game because of it.

At primary school, I hadn't been able to get into the school team. The odd game I did play at scrum-half, I got battered. I thought 'What am I playing this game for? It's too hard for me'. I was a bit of a coward - I didn't like the crack you got playing, it hurt and I didn't want to play. At that time, there were a lot of good players around. There were kids at school who were quicker than me and had a lot of skill and they never did anything. I wanted to be a rugby player; they've probably gone on and done great in other fields. At the time, there were a lot of hard players too, Widnes was a violent town and Rugby League was a violent game. When they say it's violent now, they should have tried living in Widnes in those days; they'd bite your ear off.

I had never lost a race in the swimming baths ever, but being house captain at Fisher Moore, I pretty much had to play rugby. We had no scrum-half, so I was asked to play there - and I didn't want to play there at all. I wanted to play loose-forward.

I played at scrum-half and we won the competition. The teacher told me: 'You're a good player'. I asked him if he really thought that, and he told me that he knew it. If you think you are a good player, you are. But I hadn't finished growing and it was a very brutal game.

Outside school, I went down to a team called St Paul's and we did well. Then the vicar came and complicated matters. You've got to remember that in those days what Widnes was like: Catholic and Protestant, Labour and the Tories, it was a war. My mum used to say: 'Here's the rotten eggs and tomatoes' when the Tories came round canvassing for votes and you used to throw them at their cars.

My mum was an out-and-out Labour voter. My dad told me never to vote Tory because I'd never want to see the days where you queued waiting for a man to die in order to get a job. Those words stay with you, especially from your dad. If I got caught talking to a Protestant, that was it, I was out of the house. My dad said to me one day: 'Where have you been?' and I said: 'I've been seeing my brother - your son'.

My brother was courting a Protestant at the time, so my dad chucked me out of the house. I slept on a park bench for three nights. I was only 15 at the time. He had to chuck me out though, because I did tell him she had nice legs!

I had served my time as an apprentice to become a painter and decorator, but was glazing for the Corporation at the time. I had to stay out of the house for three days until my dad had cooled down. I was a Catholic, so with several others I had to leave St Paul's and form our own amateur team, Lowerhouse. We won 18 from 18 matches.

I'd only played about three games for my new side when I was told that Widnes wanted to sign me. My coach at the time, Jackie Hayes, was a former Widnes player and he went down to the club with me for a meeting. They said in the meeting: 'You get soft money here, look at Jackie, he wasn't good enough to play for St Helens and he got soft money here'. I didn't like the way they spoke about Jackie as he had helped me, and here they were calling him so I told them to stick it.
Widnes told me had ruined my career before it had started but I didn't think I had. I thought if that's the way they are, I don't want to sign for them.

7

After that, I played in a public trial; first team forwards and 'A' team backs. I ran through the Widnes pack twice and scored, thinking: 'That will show 'em'.

I carried on playing in amateur Rugby League and Saints wanted to sign me. They asked me what I wanted and I told them I wanted £500. They said you've got that plus another £500 when you've played six first team games. I went to my dad and told him I was signing for St Helens in the morning.

2. Douggie's a Saint

I remember my first training session at St Helens after I signed in 1962. I took three buses, two in Widnes and changed again outside Rainhill Mental Hospital. I had my kit bag; in those days you took all your own gear. I walked down the road, across the training pitch and into Knowsley Road on my tod. I enquired of some gentleman 'Where do I report for training?' 'Into the 'A' team dressing room,' I was told. I was 11 stone four pounds and knew nobody in there. I think Frank Barrow asked: 'Are you in the right place cocker?' Even the accent was totally different; they all seemed so much older and bigger than me. I hadn't even started shaving. Then it was on with the kit and down the players' tunnel. Wow. As a speccy I had watched Murphy, Vinty, Huddart and van Vollenhoven on that turf.

My first game for Saints was in the 'A' team against Workington. My dad had told me they were hard men up in Cumbria. I remember going into the dressing room to put my stuff on the peg and I had to jump up to reach it! I thought 'How big are this lot?' Going to Cumbria was always hard; a few players would pick up mysterious injuries just before trips to one of the Cumbrian sides. I think that sometimes even Murph wasn't too keen on playing up there. It was a big deal all round for me, I had just signed for St Helens who were the top side in the game at the time and I knew it was going to be a step up from what I was used to. The pitch was like a bog, and during the game, one of their forwards, Martin hit me and loosened my tooth. I started to shout at him, he punched me again and knocked the tooth back in. I thanked him.

I was constantly being told that I would never make it at loose-forward, because I wasn't big enough. There was no team weight training in the game at that time. What you had instead was the library. Steve Llewellyn was the 'A' team coach at Saints at that time, the man who had scored that fabulous try I had seen as a kid was now my coach. He wanted to know why I wasn't playing centre and I explained I was going to be a loose-forward or nothing. He told me to go to the library and look for books on weight training. I remember reading the first book I found about weight training. It said that Hercules wanted to lift a bull over his head. He tried to do it, but couldn't. So what he did was find a calf and lifted that over his head and continued to do so every day as the calf grew until eventually the calf became a bull and Hercules was at last able to lift a bull over his head. That's still the secret of weight training. The best saying in coaching is: 'It's no good being able to lift the bull over your head if you can't catch it'. I wanted to get bigger, but I also wanted to make sure that no one would be able to catch me. I wanted to be the best.

As soon as Saints came in for me I thought 'I could be playing with Alex Murphy, Tom van Vollenhoven and Dick Huddart.' The names just rolled off your tongue. Vinty had gone to Widnes by then and I thought: 'I've got to play against my idol.' I did eventually get to play against Vinty and I was in awe of him. To be fair, he hit me with that big tackle he had, but he didn't put everything behind it, he didn't clean me out. So I thought 'I'll do the same'. When I played against Harry Pinner much later in my career I went into tackle him and didn't give him the full hit. Vinty was gentle with me really, which was nice. He probably thought I was a bit of an upstart walking in his stride, but when he tackled me, he could have hurt me and he didn't. That was the kind of man he was, and it made think that I would never hurt a kid playing the game when I got older.

First team debut

I didn't stay in the 'A' team too long and my debut for the first team was against Liverpool City in a pre-season charity match. In the first team, I did all right, and at the time I used to read everything written about me in the newspapers. As you get older you tend to think 'stuff 'em' and you get blasé about reports. As a kid though, you read everything written about you and take on board everything the coach says to you. You've got to remember a coach can destroy a kid by saying the wrong thing to him as well as help him on his way by saying the right things.

I remember I played my fifth game for the first team at Featherstone. I was five yards out from my own line and got hit by one of their forwards and ended up slamming against the brick wall behind the line. I thought 'that's it, I'm finished'. I told my dad that the game was too hard for me. I told him that I wasn't prepared to get killed playing Rugby League. I thought my back had been broken; it still aches now. My dad told me that I should still go next week, because that would entitle me to the remaining £500 on my contract and give me a start in life. So I turned up again the next week and I thought to myself that I wasn't going to do a thing on that pitch, I was going on just to get my money and then that was it, I was finished with the game. I thought everyone was to blame for what had happened, that the game had nearly broken my back and I hated everyone at that time because I was a kid. This was subsequently to help me as a coach, because if I ever saw a young player feeling down, I would tell him he was a great player and try to build up his confidence. Looking back at that time, no one spoke to me, the strong survived and that was it. You might have lost 10 Doug Laughtons and even Alex Murphys to the game.

During the next game, I was standing on the pitch and Murph said to me, bearing in mind this is a book likely to be read by families, I have adapted the quote slightly: 'You lazy punt Laughton, clucking run'. He gave me the ball and I went the length of the field to score. 'Same again young 'un?' he asked and later 'This could go on all day.' That was it, I was a star. You'd have thought I'd done everybody's tackling for them; I was praised to the highest heavens. All the hard work in the previous games and the papers said nothing, I never got a mention. Suddenly, I'd done nothing in a game, stood there picking my nose and scratching my arse until Murph told me to run. I was quick, but it was Murph who saved my career. That day I thought I was playing my last match, but he sent me in for a try, turned to me and said: 'You're doing alright now, I'm going to make you a good player', and he did.

The thing that made Murphy great was his attitude and his dedication to the game. I would never be late for training, but Murphy would be there a couple of hours before everybody else. Put the boots on, that's all he wanted to do, and play Rugby League. He was amazing, he could tell you what was going to happen during a game before it happened. He was the best ever. Every kid looked up to Alex even though he wasn't that much older than me. I remember the first final I reached with Saints: the 1964 Lancashire Cup Final, I asked Alex before the game if we were going to win. He said from the first scrum if Harvey catches the pass that Alex was going to give him, we'll win. From the first scrum, Alex set up a try underneath the sticks. The other thing I thought about Alex was that he didn't like anybody having the same bottle as him. I felt he was the big 'I am'. However, you can't be big headed if you've done it though.

I wouldn't say he was kind to kids, but he was never bad to kids. He'd tell you what you needed to know; he was just so devoted to the game. The other great player I have seen is Wally Lewis and if you could have put them together you never would have lost. Murph could kick a dustbin lid further than Barry John, the legendary Wales Rugby Union number 10. When they changed the rules so that drop goals were only worth one point Murph just said: 'I'll kick twice as many'. I don't know how he used to kick those heavy balls. They were made of leather and felt like they weighed half a ton, especially when wet.

In those days and often still now, there was the first team and the 'A' team which were very separate entities at the club. However, Dick Huddart took the time to speak to me while I was in the 'A' team. He told me he had watched me play and that I was going to do all right. Once I had got into the first team, we were due to play in a big match. I went out with Dick the Saturday before the match after we had played earlier that day, and found myself sitting in a jazz club in Liverpool on the Monday! I remember saying to him: 'Dick I've got to get back to training'. He told me not to worry and that I would be playing. I finally got back to Saints and Stan McCormick, the coach, dropped me. I walked out of the ground but later read the paper to see that Dick was still playing and there was no Laughton. I spoke to Dick and he said: 'I'm not playing if you're not playing'. The outcome was that the directors informed me they had spoken to Dick who had told them that if I wasn't playing he would be out of the building never to return and consequently I was back in the team. I thought to myself that that would be the end of McCormick at the club, but was grateful that Dick had taken me under his wing.

Spending two days with him in a jazz club having a few drinks wasn't ideal preparation for a match though. I kept saying 'Dick I'm knackered, I want to go home'. What a madman! He was a great player though and had no fear of anything. Most Rugby League forwards of that era were the same. I got to that mentality myself eventually. Once the penny drops, you just think no one is going to knock anymore of your teeth out without you doing the same to them. That's the hard bit. You just learnt to live with the violence by becoming violent yourself. You used to be coached to hit people with your forearm. The old maxim was: 'They can't go without their heads'. That's gone out of the game now and that's how it should be. The game is better for the relative absence of violence now. It's still a hard game, but far less violent and I wouldn't want it back.

One player broke my jaw and I waited for my opportunity to play against him again and exact some revenge. I didn't care whether the form my revenge would take was contrary to the rules of the game, I just wanted to make him suffer. That's how bad it was, we were a violent lot. I remember once being at a bar after I had been named captain of Lancashire. I was wearing my blazer with the captain's badge on it and someone started giving me trouble. I thought to myself 'you are not going to damage this blazer'. I had so much pride in it because I was captaining a side that contained the likes of Murphy and Myler. I hit the bloke once, his head hit the bar and he was out cold.

Once I became tougher, people realised that they didn't hit Doug anymore because he'd hit you back. It was the same elsewhere. You didn't hit Warrington's Mike Nicholas because he was tough and you don't mess with big Jim Mills or you could be hospitalised. Instead, you hit the people who didn't hit you back. Looking back, it could be argued that we were bullies. I wasn't that way to start with, but the game made

12

me a bully. You either became a bully or got bullied. If someone hit you, you hit them back. It happened again and again until eventually you left each other well alone and you targeted the soft players instead. It was easier. I know that sounds vicious but it was.

I visited Zimbabwe and while I was there a man got his arm cut off as he was being robbed. I'm told it's one of the most violent places on earth and you're more likely to get done there than anywhere else. Well you can go to the pub at the bottom of my road to get done, but they probably won't cut your arm off, it would be an exception, but being in Rugby League at that time means nothing violent shocks you much.

My first sending off was at Rochdale Hornets for persistent offside. From memory it was around 1964. It was a horrible, freezing, sleeting night. Rochdale had recruited three Fijians. One, the winger, ran over our winger, went back and ran over him again. The Fijian hooker had a head like a cement bucket, and our front row were all bleeding. The second rower, a giant of a man, was knocking us flying. I thought that he was like a snowball coming down the mountain and my best option was to fly up and meet him before he got going; hence the persistent offside. In the bath afterwards I remarked to Ray French that the second rower's thighs were bigger than my shoulders.

Working and earning

At first I was a painter and decorator for the local council. Then I started my own central heating business together with a brickie. Again, a book from the library helped me out. I was buying my own house and was amazed at what people were charging to fit central heating and how easy it looked. I just thought 'I could do that' just as long as the bloke I set it up with would brick up the old coal fire. After a visit to the library, we were soon doing about 15 central heating jobs a week.

The money playing Rugby League at the time was poor. You got £25 for a win and £5 for a loss. Some got a bit more. There was no chance of making your living just playing Rugby League. All it got you was a slightly better house. I loved it though. I'd do it again tomorrow. If God offered me the choice of living until I was 90 or having another 10 years of playing the game I'd take the 10 years. I just wanted to win.

There were other perks though. We were fearless; we used to dive in the weir that a chemical company now owns. You would dive in and surface about half a mile downstream. I don't know how we didn't drown. We had nothing else to live for anyway. Now the big decision is who you're going to leave your house and money to - what a load of rubbish.

13

Painter and decorator – my first job

The average game day would go like this. Say you were playing Workington away. I would have to get up early, because I would have to get myself to St Helens Town Hall from Widnes. Then you would have a six hour coach journey with no proper motorways in those days, just winding roads. Then you'd arrive about an hour before kick off, walk off the coach, knowing you were going to get physically battered because they were all big lads up there. You would get home about midnight. Twenty five quid for all that! But there was the camaraderie of men and also the laughs we sometimes had. I remember when we were on the coach going to Workington on the old roads. I wondered what the rush was as the coach driver was going hell for leather and taking corners on two wheels. We used to stop for steak and eggs in Keswick before the game. There was this little pokey betting shop down a back street there. It wasn't as big as my lounge. One of the lads had got a tip and suggested I put £20 on this horse, I thought that was a bit much because I was only on £3.50 a week at work then. I just put a fiver each way on. Anyway, it won;

I think it was 100 to 6 odds. The bookie couldn't afford to pay us out because the whole team had backed this horse. He said: 'I'll have to go home to get the money for you from my safe'. Ray French put his leg across the counter and said: 'No, you stay here and send your assistant to get the money because we don't trust you'. I just thought: 'How are we going to win a rugby game with all this going on?' He paid out a lot of money that day and all I know the next time we stopped in Keswick the betting shop wasn't there, I think we cleaned the poor bugger out.

I remember a Saints player called Goddard came in once selling shirts and one of our leading players said: 'I'll have two'. Goddard asked for payment and the player replied: 'No, they're mine'. One thing I have noticed is even though they are very well paid, today's players don't seem as happy as we were back then. I don't see many smiles on television now. One difference is this: within reason, we could say what we liked, after all what was the club going to do; stop our contracts? Now though, if you're on big money you want to safeguard that and understandably keep your mouth shut and do as you are told.

Pre-season

When I was a kid at Saints I used to do pre-season training with John Warlow, a former top Welsh Rugby Union forward. We went to Llanelli and I remember flogging up and down the beach and him standing on the sand dunes watching me and laughing. I said: 'it's alright for you, they've paid a lot of money for you, I've got to do it the hard way.' He said: 'You'll get in the side'. This pre-season was my first full season and I wanted to be as fit as I could so I could cement my place in the first team. When we'd been out for a beer Warlow used to say: 'Tell my mam we've been to the pictures'. She said to me one day 'Douggie, you must have seen every picture twice', and I replied 'We've seen one four times'. She just winked; she knew what was going on. Going to Llanelli in those days was about a seven-hour ride. With Warlow being a Welsh lad we'd be singing all the way down. It was a big adventure at the time especially with everyone there speaking Welsh. Everyone stopped Warlow in the street, he was a hero. Everywhere you went people would say: 'Best of luck up North' to him. It was quite an eye-opener really.

Early on in my Saints career, before I had even turned 21, I was placed on the transfer list for £10,000, which would have been a world record at the time. I forget what caused this but I do know that I asked to leave the club. This was typical for me, I had itchy feet already. Then we got to Wembley in 1966. The coach Joe Coan said to me 'I am going to play you in the derby game at Wigan, if you are over your knee injury I promise you I'll play you at Wembley'. I had sustained my injury by chasing a high kick from our South African winger Len Killeen on a miserable, wet night at Knowsley Road. Len kicked from the wing to the goal posts. I chased the high ball, ran on, but slid into the padding on the bottom of the goal post, which they used to whitewash with lime making the padding seem like concrete. My kneecap broke in two but I didn't know at the time, it was eight weeks later that I found out. By half-time at Wigan I knew my knee was knackered and I didn't have a chance for Wembley. The club offered to take me there with someone at the club who nobody liked. At the end of the day, if I wasn't going there to play, I wasn't going at all.

Referees

With me being a rebel, people have often wondered about my relationship with referees while I was a player. Eric Clay, the 'Sergeant Major' referee, once called me over and asked me my name. 'Laughton', I said and he promptly replied that he had never effing heard of me and furthermore I should go forth and multiply. But I always got on well with the referees; I've always thought they have a job to do. Some of them shouldn't have been given the job in the first place but that's not their fault, that's down to the people who gave them the job. It's a hard job and not something I would want to do even if you paid me £5,000 a game. It must be like being a Christian in the Coliseum in front of the baying hordes chanting 'kill'.

People have asked me in the past who was the best coach I worked under at Saints and the answer is always the same, the best coach is always the one who picks me. I worked under different styles of coaches at Saints. Stan McCormick used to like playing tick and pass in training because he was still a good player. Joe Coan, a former teacher, took to me for some reason and told me that I was the most honest kid at the club. He said: 'Don't get drawn into the other lot'. But I had just left school, had hated it and didn't want another teacher. He got me into my central heating though. Also, he played one off against the other at the club to great effect. He played Prosser off against Murphy and Murph fell for it. He did that to prove a point and be the boss, I thought he was on thin ice playing games with Murph and told Joe so. He wondered why I was the only one to bring it up with him. You know *the Emperor's New Clothes*? Well I was always the kid to say 'He's got no clothes on'. I can't see the point in being any other way. Joe wanted me to come to training from

Widnes on Sunday mornings. I said that I couldn't because I had no car and I had had my motorbike taken off me. So I had to run from Widnes, train and then run back. That took some doing especially because I was a leader in the training sessions. Joe said that everyone would look to the kid who was doing well in training and see how much he would put in to get in the side. He felt that was good for the team to see, as he wanted them to put the same in as me. It was good psychology from Joe, I respected the man. I trained very, very hard. I had set my goal of being the best and worked my arse off to achieve it. I would stand for hours throwing a rugby ball at a wall to improve my skills; every aspect of my game would be worked on. I might have had a gift but I worked at it like nobody else. I used to practice my long balls for hours.

I remember I went to the christening of one of Bobbie Goulding's children and afterwards I was talking to Paul Sculthorpe. He asked me if I was any good as a player and I said I could prove it and asked for a mark to be put on a tree. He couldn't hit it with a pass, but I did every time, both left and right. I hope he probably can now. I used to practice doing it for hours as a kid though. I used to think that if you were in a pressure situation during the game, the more knowledge you had of how far your long ball could go would help you out greatly.

Having broken my kneecap at Saints, of the five years I was at the club, I spent two years in and out of hospital. That injury should have ended my career; in those days no one came back from a broken kneecap. It was the worst injury I ever had including a broken jaw. It got to the point where I nearly lost my leg. I got back though and played one game for them. They had given me nothing while I had been injured. I had just got married, had a mortgage and was basically on my arse. I feel that Saints treated me like a piece of meat. After my first game back I was offered £25 by a board member. I told him to put it behind the bar for the lads; I was insulted by the offer. He said 'you need this don't you?' I told him I didn't need it and knew I wanted out of the club. He said that he could hang my boots from the goalposts. Then Wigan came in for me and I needed to show them I could play for Saints because if my knee was no good the move wouldn't happen. I played and the same board member at Saints said afterwards 'You've not lost it'. Again, I picked up on this as a coach. You know as a coach that when a player is low that is the time they need you most. It costs you nothing to be nice. They might be a great player you want back or they might just be a nice kid. The players who are flying high don't need you; it's the ones that are struggling that do. They're still part of your team and they're the ones that make your team great. As good as Murph was, he couldn't do it on his own.

It was an honour to sign for Saints, I wouldn't have missed Dick Huddart for the world, and loved the likes of Tommy van Vollenhoven, Wilf Smith and all those people. Voll was a lovely man and a great winger, but I think the best right winger I have ever seen in my life was Billy Boston, although I rate Voll, Martin Offiah and Brian Bevan. I played against Bevan when he was in his forties in a testimonial match. He was still like a ghost; you couldn't lay a hand on him even then. But Boston used to kill centres in defence so for me it would be Boston picked first on the right wing. What should be noted is Brian, Tommy and Billy were all right wingers which means when they were going down the wing, players tackling them were invariably using their left arm whereas with Martin Offiah being a left winger he was running onto people's stronger right arm which makes his scoring feats even more outstanding. Boston right wing, Offiah left seems pretty awesome to me. Billy was fast and strong, when you had the ball you wouldn't go anywhere near his side of the field because he would flatten you.

Moving to Wigan

Wigan had agreed to pay Saints about £6,000 for me, I think. I told Saints it would have to be £4,000 because I wanted some money off Wigan and I definitely wanted some money out of Saints. I was sitting in Harry Cook's Ford Zephyr and he offered me £250, saying that was all he had to offer me. I told him it was a grand or nothing. So he went into his other pocket and pulled out another £250 and said that was all he had to offer me. I thought he said that the first time so again stated I wanted a grand. He pulled out another £250 and said that was the bottom line. I finally believed him. I said to him 'Mr Cook I like you and I know you like me, I'm out of the club'. As I hugged him I checked all his pockets just to see if he did in fact have another £250. I took the £750 and did my deal with Wigan. It's not a back hander, if they'd not paid the tax on it that's their business. Saints made a good profit on me at the end of the day. The move finally took place on 16 May 1967.

To be honest, I didn't really want to play the game after what had happened at Saints. I had been hurt by how I felt I had been treated. They had made me feel like a used car that was no good any more. Don't get me wrong, they had given me as much as I had given them, but the way I feel I was treated while seriously injured left a lot to be desired.

18

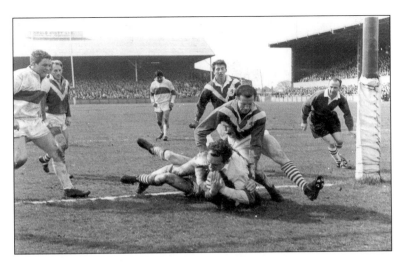

Top: Doug Laughton watches (far left) as prop John Tembey scores a try against Swinton at Knowsley Road on Saturday 19th April 1965.
The home side won 16-5. (Photo: Courtesy Alex Service)

Bottom: Kings of Lancashire!
Saints line up with the Lancashire Cup (left) and Lancashire League trophies at Knowsley Road during the 1964-65 campaign. Back row: Keith Northey, John Warlow, Kel Coslett, Ray French, Doug Laughton, Wilf Smith; Bob Burdell; Front row: Cen Williams, Tom van Vollenhoven, John Tembey, Alex Murphy, Len Killeen, Peter Harvey. (Photo: Courtesy Alex Service)

Top: Mackeson Competition Winners 1964-65. Saints line up with their commemorative tankards at Knowsley Road. Back row: Cliff Watson, Ray French, Mervyn Hicks, Doug Laughton, John Tembey, Bob Dagnall, John Warlow, Billy Benyon; Front row: Len Killeen, Frank Barrow, Keith Northey, Alex Murphy, Joe Egan, Cen Williams, Peter Harvey. (Photo: Courtesy Alex Service)

Bottom: Saints at Training 1965-66, with League Leaders Bowl, Lancashire League and Lancashire Cup trophies. The Challenge Cup was to arrive shortly. Back row: Cen Williams, John Warlow, John Mantle, Cliff Watson, Bob Dagnall, Doug Laughton, Ray French, Mervyn Hicks, Dave Wood, Frank Barrow; Front row: Tom van Vollenhoven, Wilf Smith, Bob Prosser, Alex Murphy, Peter Harvey, Billy Benyon, Len Killeen. (Photo: Courtesy: Alex Service)

3. Wembley at last

When I got out of my car at Central Park in May 1967 (yes in the five years I had been playing we now all had cars) I remember thinking 'You're not a kid anymore, you're 23 years old, you even shave twice a week'. The first person to greet me was coach Eric Ashton, another of my boyhood heroes. He said 'welcome to the Mecca'. My first impression at Wigan was that St Helens was a rugby town; Wigan on the other hand was a rugby mad town.

Wigan were really struggling at the time I joined them having lost high calibre players like Eric Ashton, Roy Evans and Brian McTigue; they were rebuilding. I had good years there though and we got there in the end. The difference between Saints and Wigan was that Wigan taught me to read the game, although they didn't have as good a side as Saints. It was a difference place; they just didn't have the quality that Saints had. I felt that Wigan had tried to do things on the cheap and signed some bad players as a result. Saints had a cracking pack full of hard lads but at Wigan, Colin Clarke and I were the only international prospects. I enjoyed my stay at Wigan though because although we weren't that good we always gave Saints a hard time when we played them. When I had played for Saints in the Saints - Wigan derbies at Knowsley Road, there would very often be gates of 25,000, but when I went to Wigan they were struggling to get 11,000 for the same game.

I loved playing at Wigan because the pitch was a bit wider which really suited my style of play. I hear people today telling forwards simply to drive forward, this amazes me. Why not do what we did and stretch a side's defence from one side of the pitch to the other rather than waiting for the opposition to set their defence and plod towards them accepting the tackle. I learnt at Wigan to work it so you had numbers on your opponents in attack by moving the ball away from where most of their defence was. I didn't learn it at Saints. The Wigan coach, Eric Ashton, taught me how to play rugby. What Ash called the golden rule in the game was that if somebody made a break, the defence would chase them and be stuck in that area of the field. So what you did next was to spread the ball across to the other side of the field and stretch their defence. If you don't score at that side, switch it back again and tire out their defence. That was one of the most valuable lessons I ever learned. I used to coach that way myself.

Ash was terribly superstitious, but he was also a nice man and a great player in his day. He was one of the greatest centres I have ever seen. When people say you don't have to be a big name to be a coach I hear what they are saying, but I think you are more likely to take on board what a great of the game is telling you to do. I'm not saying just because you are a great player it will make you a great coach but I think it does give you an advantage.

Once at Wigan I was chasing an opposing winger Bill Burgess, who was a real flyer. I missed him by a couple of inches and afterwards in the bar a supporter approached me and told me where he had felt I had gone wrong. He told me how I could have caught Burgess by changing the angle of my run and even had I not caught him he would only have scored in the corner making the conversion harder. His advice was right and I told him so because I listened to supporters. Just because you're a speccie doesn't mean you can't read a game. I've probably picked up more tips from speccies than I have from players or coaches. It's the willingness and ability to learn that make you better. I know for a fact that I was a better coach at the end of my career than I was when I started.

Experiencing an upbringing where having a chicken for tea was big news does make you appreciate things more when you do get them. I remember I had my first fillet steak through playing rugby for Wigan. I'd hurt my tooth during the game and couldn't eat but after the game we were taken to a restaurant. I was determined not to miss out on the fillet steak so I wrapped it up and swiftly introduced it to my jacket pocket. Later we went onto the casino and someone said to me: 'Something smells good in your pocket'. I said: 'It's fillet steak, my mam'll get four dinners out of this'. One of my team mates said 'I'll have some' and he received the customary two-word reply to his request because he had eaten his.

It was like that at Wigan though, they were always a bit above Saints in that respect. They thought like Leeds used to do, that they would look after the players in different ways. Actually I just wanted to be paid more, then I would be happy. I thought: 'Don't offer me champagne when I want beer, give me my money', so that approach never worked with me.

We had what was known as 'The Big Three' at Wigan, these three cheerleaders of wholesome proportions. The lads said that we should get rid of them because they were a bit embarrassing, but Ash was so superstitious he said: 'I was going to get rid of them but if they're not at that end you don't score' pointing to one end of the pitch. I pointed out to him that they changed ends at half time. We had this kid at Wigan, Ronnie Webb, who had never scored for the club and at that time Wigan had a big bath, as big as my front room and about eight feet deep, it was massive. When you scored, you had to tell the story of your try and run the team through it when in the bath. Ronnie scored his first try one day and I asked him to run us through it. He said 'It was like this Douggie. I got the ball and I could see The Big Three in front of me and I thought if the gap is that big I can get through it'.

Prop forward Geoff Fletcher signed for Wigan in 1967. I could write a chapter on him alone. In those days Fletcher would pay no more than £50 for a car so instead I used to pick him up. One day he said: 'Don't bother picking me up today, I've got a load of stuff for the lads'. I got to training and he said: 'Put this lot in your car'. There were loads of bananas, cauliflowers and cabbages. I got into the club and he gave all the other lads loads of the stuff as well. Coming back from training, we stopped at Billinge Lump for a pint. I said: 'Geoff, what's with all the bananas and cabbages?' He said 'well, they were swill, but I thought they're too good for the pigs so I washed them down'. I got to training the next day and I asked Clarkey: 'You've not had any of them bananas yet have you?' He said: 'They were a bit green' and I told him that they were pig swill. Clarkey immediately went up to Geoff eyeballing him, irate that he had given him pig swill to eat.

One day Geoff told me that he would pick me up in his new car. I heard him tooting his horn outside and I knew I would have to get going because Geoff would become impatient. I ran outside and as I opened the door he shouted: 'don't open it'. I looked down and the door had come off in my hand.

The other thing with Geoff and with other players at Wigan that made me laugh was the team photo being taken. As soon as they had to line up, they would all be dashing off to get their toupees and false teeth. It wouldn't be so bad, but then when they played they had no hair.

There was one occasion when I had Geoff in my car and we were driving down Moss Bank Road when he said: 'Promise me you won't laugh'. I asked 'What do you mean?' He was sitting in the passenger seat and he had this sort of cake box. He just insisted that I promise not to laugh and I assured him that I wouldn't. He opened the box and pulled out this toupee and plonked it on his head. He said: 'Laughton, you promised you wouldn't laugh'. I thought it was hilarious. He asked me worriedly: 'what do you think the lads will do when they see it?' and I replied: 'I think they'll laugh'. We got to training and one of the lads put silver balls in it as if it was a bird's nest. He stayed at Wigan until 1974.

Another character was Stuart Wright, who started his career for Wigan in 1969. I noticed during the games he kept on going to the bench to have a word with Eric Ashton. I spoke to Ash about it: 'Every week this fellow comes over to you during the game, I'm the skipper, what's he saying?' Ash replied: 'He keeps saying "How am I doing?"' He was a good winger though.

Meeting the board

I wanted Wigan to sign Dave Robinson, the Great Britain loose-forward so Eric Ashton said: 'Well, where are you going to play?' I said: 'You're the boss; I'll play anywhere you want'. He told me that Wigan would have to pay £10,000 for him which was a lot of money in those days. I said: 'We need him Ash; the pack is not good enough, get the pack sorted, help the backs out'. I'd played second-row on tour and told Ash I would play there and if I had got it wrong, it was my own doing. So we stood outside the boardroom and I could hear from inside the chairman with the big cigar bang down his hammer and declare the meeting open. What followed was the strangest half hour of my life.

Chairman: 'Reet, what's first on t' agenda lads? The groundsman Billy Mitchell's lawnmower'

On the left: 'What's up with his lawnmower?'

Chairman: 'He says it won't cut t' grass.'

On the right: 'Well, I've had same lawnmower for 20 years and it cuts t' grass fine.'

On the left: 'Is your lawn as big as Central Park though?'

Chairman: 'Come on lads, get real. Do we get new blades, have it sharpened or buy him a new lawnmower?'

On the right: 'I suppose the lazy bugger wants one you can sit on.'

On the left: 'Central Park is a big area and there's the training pitch also.'

On the right: 'I repeat, there's nowt up with it; it only needs sharpening.'

Well this went on for 20 minutes until the chairman asked if they could come to a decision on whether to have the blades sharpened, have new blades fitted or buy a new lawnmower. There was no way they were buying a new lawnmower so they decided to have the blades sharpened because they didn't want to be throwing money away. Next thing, Eric the coach went in. In those days at Wigan, the coach had to report back to the board and say how each player had played in the previous game. It was correct in a way because they used to write it all down so the coach couldn't come back the next week and say the same thing. It was a bit like that at Leeds when I was manager. Anyway, the next thing that happens is old Mary took some celery into the meeting. Ash knew that I was listening and as soon as he started to speak the board members all started chomping on the celery.

'Eric, you're not saying anything lad,' said one director.

'I can't hear myself speak over the celery,' replied Ash.

Captain of Wigan

I was giggling at this point outside the door. Eventually Eric made himself heard and said: 'Douggie wants us to sign this Dave Robinson'.
'Who's he?'
'Well, he's the current Great Britain loose-forward.'
'How much do we need to pay?'

So Eric told them £10,000 and they asked him to step outside while they discussed the matter. Not even two minutes had passed before they called Eric back in to agree a record signing. They spent 20 minutes on a lawnmower! I thought I'd never be a coach if this is what you had to deal with. Mind you, one of the directors was so blind he had to paint his gatepost white to get into his drive. Those sort of things made Wigan funny. I thought 'I can run rings round this lot'.

Every year at Wigan, all the pub sides would play in what was known as the Ken Gee Cup on the pitch at Central Park. In 1968, Eric Ashton said to me 'There's this kid playing and he's six foot four and looks like he's a cracker'. I watched him play, agreed that he was a good player and we decided that he would be signed. He was in the first team four weeks after, his name was Bill Ashurst. He had been like the Excalibur sword sticking out saying 'Get me out of here'. We had found such a great player out of a competition like that. He played at Wigan until 1977, played 179 games, scoring 152 goals.

I thought to myself 'there's another lesson': watch as many players as you can, get them all in one place and find one Ashurst, it's worth a fortune. We had signed Dave Robinson, already had me and completed the back three with Ashurst. He could kick a dustbin lid further than not only Barry John, but Murphy as well. Ashurst was the best kicker in open

25

play I have ever seen, he always used to curl the ball in just by the corner flag and never missed. He had unreal talent. If I had had him when I first started coaching I truly believe I would have made him the greatest player you ever saw. He was certainly a world-class forward and we now had a formidable back three; Ashurst, Robinson and Laughton. They used to pair them in threes in Wigan in those days, Boston, Ashton and McTigue not that I am comparing us with them though. We went a year without being beaten and Wigan gave us a watch each for this accomplishment. They said if we didn't lose for another year we could get two watches. I've always hated the carrot being placed in front of me. Don't dangle it in front of me, I'm not a donkey.

I learnt about managing players as well. I remember Eric Ashton saying to me that one player was causing problems and that he had brought his gas bill in saying he wanted the club to pay it or he wouldn't play. I told him that he must realise that if the club paid it once for him it would be paying it every week. Eric said 'What can I do' and I just said 'Do what you've got to do'. What I would have done is give him the money once and tell him that if he ever tried it again he would be out the door. I always used to think that if you could see the problem coming, get it before it gets you, stop it in its' tracks. From that point on the player brought every bill to the club.

The 1970 Challenge Cup Final

I had an office in Nutgrove when I was playing at Wigan and one of the women said there was someone there to see me. This fellow had one of those hard briefcases which were rare in those days. While he was talking to me he began lifting the briefcase towards me. He said to me he was doing a story on Wigan for a newspaper and with me being the captain of the club he thought he would talk to me. It turned out that the reason for his visit was that instead of the club sacking the secretary, they had left him there working his notice so he had gone through the books and he'd sold his story to one of the Sunday nationals. My visitor was recording what I was saying through his briefcase, so I just started moving further and further away from him and told him all kinds of rubbish.

As soon as he'd gone I rang the club and said I was sure that someone from one of the Sunday papers had been talking to me. The response I got was that I must be imagining things. I assured them I didn't imagine things and that I had been asked if I received backhanders when the team won. In any case, these are not illegal payments as it turned out; they're only illegal if you don't pay the tax on them. Shortly afterwards, a

26

barrister from London appeared at a board meeting. He came out afterwards and said to me that if it went to court, I was the only person he would take, not any of the board members.

This was all happening during Wembley week of 1970 and I'd been told that the headline the paper concerned was going to use was that the man who leads Wigan out at Wembley is a crook. I thought I don't like that as I was skipper, but in fact it was the chairman they were trying to set up. The newspaper did run the story, but the club didn't get into trouble over the payments. It was a tax issue, there was no 'scandal'.

Here I was close to realising my dream of lifting the Challenge Cup at Wembley and there's all this crap going on. I was thinking 'there's no more than about 60 odd players who have lifted the Challenge Cup and I want to be one. This is my dream, all the training, injuries, now this crap plus our opponents in the Final, Castleford, will be tough.' Off we went for the cup. The game was notorious for Colin Tyrer breaking his jaw in a terrible, off the ball, incident caught on camera by the large army of photographers. We were up against what was probably the best Castleford team anyone has seen. They had a very tough pack of forwards, including Denis Hartley and Mal Reilly - you don't find many tougher than those. They also had two of the finest half-backs in Keith Hepworth and Alan Hardisty. Those four players and full-back Derek Edwards were on the 1970 Lions tour with me. It is probably true to say that I learned more about football in those 10 weeks on tour with Hardisty, than I had done in the previous eight years. He really was a genius on the tactics of the game.

I never slept the night before Wembley. I was rooming with coach Eric Ashton and he was up smoking all night. He was keeping me awake, so I told him to go to sleep. He said: 'I'm the coach'. I replied: 'Well I'm your captain and I want some sleep'. He used to get very nervous though before games. Before that final, I thought 'I've finally got to Wembley, I can finally lift that cup' but I didn't. Whether I got a knock or whether it was nerves, I can say that I honestly don't remember much about that game at all. We only got beaten 7-2 and if we hadn't have lost Tyrer, our goalkicker to injury we probably would have won it.

Incidentally, the best try I ever scored came in the 1970 Challenge Cup semi-final. I broke through, chipped the full back, picked it up with one hand and went in under the posts. I was nervous before every one of my Wembley appearances, if you're not nervous there is something wrong. I was still nervous when I coached there, not as nervous, but nervous nonetheless. It's such a big event. The other thing is when you move from the a-team to the first team you immediately notice that the pace of the game is quicker. Then, when you move up to county level that's quicker still. You get to international level and you think what the bloody hell is going on here; it's so quick. And that's how it is at Wembley.

1970 Challenge Cup Final: Castleford 7 Wigan 2

This was Wigan's 11th Wembley appearance and 15th overall in the Final. They faced the Challenge Cup holders, a Castleford side built around a solid pack and half-back combination of Alan Hardisty and Keith Hepworth.

However, Castleford's victory was marred by controversy. Wigan had taken the lead in the first minute, full-back Colin Tyrer kicking a penalty. Castleford equalised six minutes later with a Redfearn penalty, and then took the lead with a try from winger Alan Lowndes in the corner. But in the 18th minute, Tyrer caught a kick in his own half, and passed to winger Kevin O'Loughlin. A split-second later, Hepworth hit Tyrer with a high tackle. Tyrer had to be taken off, with a serious facial injury. He did not break his jaw, but had to have considerable dental work to repair the damage. Hepworth claimed that he thought Tyrer was going to kick, which is why he came in high. He was cautioned for the incident. Cliff Hill came on for Tyrer, the first time a substitute had been used in the Challenge Cup Final. Even the report in the Castleford local newspaper said that their victory was marred by this incident.

Wigan could not cover for the loss of Tyrer, who was one of the best goal-kickers in the game at that time. Two minutes after he went off, Francis missed an easy kick for Wigan. A further three Wigan penalties were kicked for touch from positions where Tyrer could have scored.

The only other score was a penalty in the second half kicked by Redfearn for Castleford. Their pack was the main force in the game, and their second-rower Bill Kirkbride won the lance Todd Trophy.

A crowd of 95,255 saw Castleford retain the Challenge Cup. Wigan did not reach Wembley again until 1984, to be beaten by a Widnes team managed by Doug Laughton.

Castleford: Edwards, Briggs, Thomas, Stenton, Lowndes, Hardisty, Hepworth, Hartley, Dickinson, Redfearn, Kirkbride, Lockwood, Reilly. Sub: Hargrave.
Scorers: Try: Lowndes. *Goals:* Redfearn (2).
Wigan: Tyrer, Jones, Francis, Rowe, Kevin O'Loughlin, Hill, Parr, Ashcroft, Birdell, Hogan, Ashurst, Robinson, Laughton. Sub: Hill
Scorer: Goal: Tyrer.

Before the Challenge Cup semi-final, the Great Britain management had picked a squad of 25 for the upcoming Ashes tour to Australia. They left a space for one loose-forward. It was a straight choice between me and my opposing loose-forward in the Cup semi-final, Wallace from Hull KR. I thought: 'I'm going then', and true enough, I got in as last man.

After three great years at Wigan my knee flared up again. The original operation I had at St Helens was ground-breaking. The surgeon had offered me three choices: remove the patella and fit a rubber one; take the top piece of the knee cap out which would leave a hole; or the long job of screwing it back together and then removing the screw six months later. I knew players with the rubber knee cap and none were ever the same again. I didn't fancy a hole so took the long job. However, it grew to a point, caused internal bleeding, and I almost lost the leg. But after plenty of hard work I was back in the game. I suppose I had hit the snake again.

I left Wigan because of my knee injury and the infamous episode of The Chairman's Turkey Dinner, a story I always enjoy telling. On our way home from an away fixture in Yorkshire, Wigan always stopped at a certain hotel for a meal. The players were given a standard dish of mixed grill, but the club chairman had to have something special, and on one occasion it was a turkey dinner. I was tired of mixed grills, so deftly intercepted the chairman's plate and was well into the turkey before the great man discovered that it was missing. He roared out to ask who had got the turkey dinner and when I owned up he was so furious he immediately shouted angrily across: 'Right, Laughton! You're going on the transfer list tomorrow.' I replied: 'It's ok by me but only if you don't ask for more than £6,000.' This is where my injured knee came in. Despite his anger over the turkey, the chairman would never have agreed to sell an established international player so cheaply, if he had not thought that my injury was one that was going to end my career. Clearly he did.

I didn't want to leave Wigan. In March 1973, Widnes offered me a grand to sign and I told Wigan if they gave me £250 I would stay, but they told me I wouldn't get a penny. Another reason I left was because Eric Ashton was packing in coaching at the club. I've always been pretty loyal to my coaches; they are like a father to you at times. Ash had been very good to me at Wigan; taught me to play the game and signed Dave Robinson when I asked him to. I knew after one game with Robinson in the side I would be moved back to loose-forward anyway and that's what happened. Ash told me that I was a crafty young bugger. I later tried to talk him into staying at the club. He was going though and I didn't know who the new coach would be. Vinty Karalius was the coach at Widnes and I knew he was alright, so decided to go to my hometown club.

29

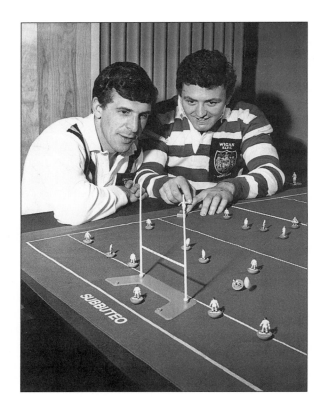

The 1970 Challenge Cup Final:
Top: With Castleford captain Alan Hardisty
Bottom: Leading out Wigan

4. The 1970 Ashes Tour

We landed in Darwin. From the moment we hit the hotel, everywhere we went, Australian supporters were chanting 'Wait till big Artie gets you!' - big Artie being the legendary great Australian forward Arthur Beetson, one of the toughest props ever and a quality player to boot.

Mind you, we all nearly killed ourselves the first day we got to Darwin. We all went for a swim in the sea when someone told us: 'No, no, no, get out, the water is full of man o' war jellyfish, they're deadly'. We were here thinking: 'Blimey, this beach is quiet; there's no-one swimming, this is great'. We stuck to the swimming pool for the rest of the tour.

As a kid, the furthest I had ever been was New Brighton on the ferry or Southport. I'd been the Isle of Man once and that had seemed like hundreds of miles away. Here I was in Australia and the bloody ants were as big as dogs. Now I was on the tour my aim was to get in the test side. Mal Reilly was the loose-forward and a good 'un too and I thought that I might have to aim for a second-row spot. I played against Queensland, which we won 32-7, and I had a good game, I think I scored three tries. I was asked if I could play second-row and replied that I could. That was it, I was in the side for the first test. What a nightmare that game was. There was a lot of fighting on both sides. We got hammered 37-15, but I managed to score. Graham Langlands scored nine goals for the Australians.

The management made a couple of changes for the second test and we took revenge, winning 28-7. In that test big Artie got me – 'king hit' off the ball. I was on the deck and asked Syd Hynes, who was stood above me: 'What hit me?' 'Big Artie got you'. Syd was only a small man compared to big Artie but he said: 'Knock the basket over Doug and I'll kick his head off'. I did and Syd did. Unfortunately, Syd later got sent off for kicking Beetson, but we still won, and scored three tries while we were down to 12 men. Roger Millward equalled an Ashes record by scoring 20 points – two tries and seven goals.

Third test

Before the last test against Australia at the Sydney Cricket Ground, there was a lot of hype about them bringing Johnny Raper back. We were going to play against a regional side that Raper would be playing in and I was talking to these two fellows back at the hotel before the game. They told me that Johnny Raper had a cut above his eye and they were hoping it wouldn't open up during the game. I told them 'it'll come open, don't worry about that'. We didn't want him back in their test side, not that it would have changed the result I don't think. Their full-back for that test, Allan McKean, was like Frano Botica. In fact he was probably a better goal kicker. He could kick them long range and of course in those days they had their own referee.

I remember that test, which was the last time Great Britain won the Ashes, very well. We scored five tries to one and won by four points: 21-17. I thought every decision went their way. We had a settled side, we were growing in confidence and the only hope the Aussies had was through their fabulous goalkicker and getting us penalised off the field.

The Aussies could only score one try against us. It was a tough game again, and in the second half Artie Beetson was sent off for punching Cliff Watson. We had some good players in that test side and a lot of commitment. I remember saying to Mal Reilly that I wanted him to take the ball into the tackle, stop, hold the ball out and I would take it off him. We never used the move in the second test and in this test they had gone ahead with about a quarter of an hour left. I said: 'We're going to have to do it'. We did it and it worked like a dream as I sent Roger Millward in under the sticks, that was the ball game and the Ashes.

I injured my nose badly in that third test, I heavily tackled one of their players, he jumped back up to have a go at me and another Aussie ran in and they both started swinging punches. Jim Thompson, one of our second rowers, ran in and grabbed hold of my arms. My head looked like it was on a coconut shy as the two Aussies swung punches at me while I shouted to Jim 'don't hold me, hit them'. I also won the Frank Hyde Award for the man-of-the-match. Our hotel was a short walk from the Stadium and I can recall to this day marching through the crowd with chest stuck out like a Bantam Cock.

We beat all the regional sides we played, except New South Wales, which was a 17-all draw. We only lost the one game on the whole of the tour, the first test in Australia.

I always liked the Aussies myself; they call you a 'Pommie basket' or something very similar anyway. The thing is I've always taken that as a term of endearment from them. They think the world of you over there. They're as close to us as people as anybody. A lot of Brits go over there and whinge about it being too hot. What do they expect?

When we got to New Zealand we went out on the juice the night before we played them and we still beat them. They just weren't up to scratch in those days. We won the test matches 19-15, 23-9 and 33-16. We won our other four matches in New Zealand, scoring 257 points.

Since then the Aussies have proved almost impossible to defeat. In fact the last club side to beat them was Widnes on 25 October 1978. I was player-coach that day and won man-of-the-match again.

Some people say Saints against Wigan games are the hardest games you'll ever play in, but Great Britain against Australia was a whole other level above that. They were very, very hard games. Afterwards though, you'd all go into the bar and have a few beers. We were expected to win at the time, although we knew it would be very hard, particularly on their turf. There was no real big deal made of it at the time, put it this way, nowhere near the fuss that would be made if Great Britain won the Ashes today. You just got off the plane and all went home. In fact, I was told I owed them £300 when I got back. Beforehand, we were told we would all have a share in the tour's profits, but it turned out the tour was in the red. Even so, I'd do it again tomorrow.

I did have my eyes well and truly opened as to Australia's future potential whilst over there. On the morning of the last Test in Sydney, our Manager, Jack Harding, was mithering that the morning after the test match three players were required to present prizes to the Sydney Youth Competition. I said at the time: 'Jack, leave that until tomorrow and let's try to win the ball game first!' Imagine my surprise when having had a wonderful night of celebrations, there was a knock on my door at 8am next morning - when I had just got into bed - to say: 'You are one of the volunteers, Doug!' I said afterwards that the quality and strength of the youngsters I had seen would mean that in years to come we would not have a hope in hell of beating Australia. I wrote in my column in the *Evening Post and Chronicle*: 'When these young kids come through we will never beat Australia again'. Their skill for their age was unbelievable and I knew we didn't have anything similar back home.

The worst thing about it all was that they had a World Cup in the September after we got back. I played in that and counted up that I had played something like 70 games in 12 months. The Australians beat us after Reilly made a mistake from the scrum and that was it. I'm not calling Malcolm, as he was a great player. Malcolm remarked that on tour there was not much between Phil Lowe, him and me for pace on tour. 'How would you know that when I was in front, but wasn't going flat out', I asked. Of course I was, but that was for me to know and him to ponder.

The 1970 Ashes Tour

First test: Australia 37 Great Britain 15
6 June 1970 at Lang Park, Brisbane

Australia: Langlands, King, McDonald, Brass, Cootes, Hawthorne, Smith, Wittenberg, Walters, Morgan, Beetson, Lynch, Coote. Subs: Thompson, Weiss.
Scorers: Tries: King (2), Morgan (2), McDonald. Goals: Langlands (9).
Great Britain: Price, Sullivan, Myler, Shoebottom, Atkinson, Hardisty, Hepworth, Chisnall, Flanagan, Watson, Robinson, Laughton, Reilly. Subs: Millward, Irving.
Scorers: Tries: Flanagan, Watson, Laughton. Goals: Price (3).

Second test: Australia 7 Great Britain 28
20 June 1970 at Sydney Cricket Ground

Australia: Laird, King, McDonald, Brass, Cootes, Hawthorne, Smith, Wittenberg, Fitzsimmons, Sattler, Coote, Beetson, Weiss. Subs: Fulton, Costello.
Scorers: Try: King. Goals: McDonald, Hawthorne.
Great Britain: Edwards, Smith, Myler, Atkinson, Millward, Hepworth, Hartley, Fisher, Watson, Laughton, Thompson, Reilly. Subs: Shoebottom, Irving.
Scorers: Tries: Millward (2), Atkinson, Fisher. Goals: Millward (7), Hynes.

Third test: Australia 17 Great Britain 21
4 July 1970 at Sydney Cricket Ground
Australia: McKean, McDonald, Fulton, Brass, King, Hawthorne, Grant, Morgan, Walters, Beetson, McCarthy, Costello, Coote. Subs: Lye, Weiss.
Scorers: Try: McCarthy. Goals: McKean (7).
Great Britain: Shoebottom, Smith, Hynes, Myler, Atkinson, Millward, Hepworth, Hartley, Fisher, Watson, Laughton, Thompson, Reilly. Subs: Hardisty, Irving.
Scorers: Tries: Atkinson (2), Hynes, Hartley, Millward. Goals: Millward (3).

Tour record:
Australia: Played: 17; Won: 15; Drawn: 1; Lost: 1. For: 496; Against: 213
New Zealand: Played: 7;   Won: 7;   Drawn: 0; Lost: 0. For: 257; Against: 75

Doug Laughton played 14 games, scoring nine tries.

5. Widnes: Realising the dream

I signed for Widnes on 6 March 1973. Here I was back in my home town club having played at St Helens and Wigan. Here I was in the 'one and nines'; the seats in the stand were railway sleepers with iron handles, no back. The dressing rooms needed doing up, the training facilities were nonexistent. The club secretary was part-time and I was not impressed. After my first training session I literally cried thinking: 'What have I done, this is definitely not a good career move'. Nine weeks down the track I asked for a move. The decision that Vinty took then probably saved my career. He just said I was not for sale, that I could take my bat home, but I wasn't for sale. I don't know how, but I knew he meant it. Still, I tested him. But in the end I decided to get on with the job. They were a cracking bunch of lads but the social side was the main priority. And, at the sake of repetition, I need to win.

If someone had said then that those would be the happiest years of my life I would not have believed him. All credit to Vinty though; he started my dream and did a marvellous job helping me to attain it.

Some 10 weeks later I remember saying to scrum-half Reggie Bowden: 'If the team doesn't start doing things the way I am telling them to, they are never going to win'. Big Jim Mills was in the Albion pub with us, because Widnes had no clubhouse in those days, after one Tuesday night training session and he said: 'We're not winning so why don't we give Douggie a go?' When I left Wigan they were fifth in the table and Widnes were five off the bottom, but we turned it round within half a season.

It took four or five games to get the side sorted. If Jim hadn't suggested giving me a go, I don't know where I would have ended up. The side had a nucleus of good players, but it was difficult to tell them how to play the game. They all used to do their own thing on the pitch. There was nothing happening. I knew how to organise, I had big Jim on a rope. He just used to say: 'Give me that ball now' and I would send it to him and away we went. Vinty made me skipper and things started happening from there.

Being coached by Vinty was interesting to say the least. I remember his team talks. He was literally bouncing around, a finger missing from an incident in a scrapyard, his Elvis hairdo, a coathanger in his jacket and those drainpipe trousers he had, practically frothing at the mouth. He would say: 'It's a big game this, we've got to win this.' He said: 'I don't want you to give 'em that and that [miming forearms and punches being thrown], I want you to give 'em that and that [instead miming head butts and kicks on the floor to an imaginary opponent]'. This was the coach. I thought that he wanted us to kick seven shades out of 'em, and all the while saliva was spraying from the corners of his mouth. I thought we had better win or he will kill us. Vinty once told Jim Mills don't short-arm tackle players, get them in a headlock and grind them. He had the Saints hooker Graham Liptrot in a headlock once and Liptrot shouted 'Jim you're killing me' and Jim just replied 'Shut up, you've always wanted to be taller'. The fun we had. When we all get together these days, we still have that camaraderie of men.

I think we were the first club to use weight training, which was organised by Vinty. In his early days as a player he had built his own gym, and had always been into weight lifting. I remember when he signed Jim Mills who was playing in Australia at the time. Big Jim turned up to his first session. As usual, we were outside, whatever the weather, lifting free weights. We had different groups of players training divided on how much a player could lift. Jim walked into the ground, picked up the heaviest equipment he could find and started doing curls. He said: 'What do I do with these?' 'Start a group on your own' we said. He was amazingly strong. He was definitely the hardest player of them all. You had to be insane to take him on.

I also remember when statistics started to come into the game. I was assistant coach to Frank Myler and Frank had been given the tackle count for each of the players. At half time he called me into the back room. 'Look at this', he said. 'Big Jim's only done one tackle in all the first half'. 'Get him told', I replied. 'Or send it in writing'. He went up to Jim and said: 'It says here you only made one tackle in the first half, how do you explain that?' Jim just replied: 'Well, would you run at me?' There was no answer to that. He was massive, but was like a flying machine too and a nice man when out of rugby kit.

I scored a hat-trick early on at Widnes against Workington. I was asked before the game if I could score three tries and I said that I could. I scored all three in the first half and at half time I was asked whether I could get another three. I told them I was bored. And it's true, I get bored very easily. Once a game had been won, once the opponents were too far behind, I just used to think: 'There's not a lot for me to do'. If it was 38-0 you would see me having a Woodbine and scratching my arse. If it was 5-5 I would be in there, trying to win the game. I needed to win; once the game was won and I knew we couldn't get beaten, I would lose a bit of interest and concentration.

One night Vinty wanted to see me, there was an 'A' team game on and I was supposed to see him at half time. I thought while I was there I might as well watch the game. The first team was struggling for forwards at the time and I saw this kid playing for our 'A' team who really impressed me. When I went to see Vinty, I told him to get this lad in the first team. He was Mick Adams, who went on to become a very good second-rower. At that time I could picture him coming onto some of the balls I sent out and it came to pass - he turned out to be a real good 'un.

Great Britain

I was made captain of Great Britain in 1974 for the match against France on 20 January in Grenoble; prior to the test series against Australia. I heard a little whisper that I was being made captain because Great Britain were expected to lose which would allow the captaincy to be taken off me and given to David Watkins in time for the Australia games. I was negotiating to go over to Australia and play with Canterbury at the time and they wanted a decision from me. I wanted to know before the France game who would captain the tour. I was told that if we got the job done against the French I would get the nod. This is how your career can be looked at like a ladder. You signed on for a professional club, that's the first rung on the ladder. You get in the 'A' team, that's another one. You get into the first team, up you go again. Then you get picked for your county, that's another step up and then you get picked for your country and you're well up the ladder by that point.

Anyway, during the game one of the French players kicked Mal Reilly up the arse so I went over to forearm him and got his teeth in my arm. Over the next few days, my arm went green. I still have the scar. They could be a dirty set of players the French, they would kick you then run off. I don't speak French but at the civic reception in front of the mayor after the game I vented my anger at having some of our side bitten and said of the team: 'Frogs? They're not frogs, they're dogs', and the interpreter happily passed this information on to the assembled throng. The mayor came over to me and offered me some wine, saying: 'You get passionate don't you?' I said that I did and it wasn't worth playing the game if you didn't get passionate over it. We hammered the French 24-5 and I was man of the match.

Prior to the return match against France at Wigan on 17 February, I asked the tour manager if I had got the tour captaincy job, but was told nothing had been decided at the moment.

Whatever, in this game at Wigan we were struggling in the first half against the French, even though we managed a 10-0 half time lead. The manager for the upcoming Australian tour came to me at half time and said 'Great players play every game to the best of their ability even when pissed off'. In the second half we murdered them and it ended up 29-0. I had a good game and scored and I asked again if I would be captain in Australia and I was told by the tour manager that if he was to keep his job I wouldn't be captain on the tour. So instead of going on the tour, I signed for Canterbury to play a short season of club Rugby League in Australia.

It was a stupid mistake. My brother used to keep a scrapbook of my career and he stopped doing it after that. The biggest disappointments in my career have always been of my own making really. I've always answered people back when I've been spoken to in what I've considered to be the wrong manner. I don't think you're good unless you feel like you're special and that sometimes makes you turn round to people and say 'you're not treating me like that' and that's when you make your mistakes, when you get on your high horse. For a while I actually carried round these hand-carved little horses with me and gave them out to people who get a bit too big for their boots. And yes, I've got my own before anyone asks. Canterbury Bankstown never did anything wrong to me, but I was cheesed off while I was there because I kept thinking that I should have been a part of the tour instead.

Bondi beach

When Canterbury signed me they told me that I would have a flat on Bondi beach and a job in a gym. But the area I actually ended up living in was an area where none of the residents seemed to have less than five kids. When I was there I was told I had to take some blokes out for a few beers in the afternoon. I couldn't drink because I had to train later so had about 12 cokes, I think I farted my way through training that day. Anyway, these blokes said to me that I should have a few beers with them after training. I made my way back, once I had finished and as I suspected they might be, they were all out for the count after the amount they had put away in the afternoon.

I didn't play many games over there because after a couple of games of the Sydney competition I did my knee ligaments. The biggest falling out I ever had as a player with a coach was with the coach at Canterbury Bankstown. Before I went I had hurt my knee and Canterbury had won about 10 games on the trot, but the coach wanted to make me captain. I said 'No, we're doing great, leave things as they are; I'm not bothered about being captain'. I never was interested in being captain as long as we won. I used to boss things out on the park anyway. We lost the next three because my arrival upset the balance of the team.

The coach had a go at me one day over only having done 16 tackles during a match, pointing out that the hooker had made 50. I just told him that I would do 70 the next week if that was what he wanted. He came in the dressing room after the next game and labelled me a genius. I had topped the tackle count but hadn't really tackled anyone at all. I just went round putting my hand on people who were being tackled. I was told it was amazing and a record tackle count.

I just replied: 'But I haven't hurt anybody'. I'd done 16 the week before, saved three tries and cleaned two players out. Then I do nothing but dance around the pitch putting my hand on people singing: 'Where do you go little one? Where do you go to dream?', and suddenly I am the best thing ever. I was always used to people being straight with me, not all this garbage of going behind my back. I just told the coach that I couldn't be doing with him or the way he did things so I just got on a plane and finished. I remember the Australian press really gave it to me, but I gave them only one quote: 'It's a question of mind over matter. I don't mind and you don't matter'.

The first thing you realise when you go to Australia is how big the game is over there. It's like Premiership football over here, all over the newspapers and television. I think their club competition at that time had a little bit of a higher standard than ours back home, say eight rungs.

I brought Chris Anderson, the current Australian coach, back over to Widnes with me as a player and he played in the Wembley Cup Final of 1975. He had played for Canterbury and Australia and was a good winger which Widnes really needed at the time.

I loved playing more than anything. Playing was everything, so success as a coach later on just wasn't quite the same as success as a player. There is nothing better than being in the middle of the park with the ball in your hands thinking 'I'm in the clear'. I remember we had a winger at Widnes called Alan Prescott who we used to refer to as 'Precious McKenzie', because he was nuts on the weights. He used to run with his knees really high and half the time his knees had more chance of getting the ball than his hands. We were playing in the 1975 Challenge Cup semi-final and Widnes hadn't been to Wembley for 11 years. It was the last minute and I made a break and saw the Wakefield full-back, Harold Box, coming for me. He wasn't quick, he wasn't slow, but he always seemed to have the correct angle on you. I kept on edging towards one side of the field and as Box hit me I threw the long ball out towards Precious. I heard someone say 'Great ball'. I said 'Never mind that, did he catch the bloody thing?' He had and we were on our way to Wembley. There is nothing like the feeling of winning a Challenge Cup semi-final because you know you are on the way to Wembley. That was also the best try that I ever made in my career.

Prior to the Final against Warrington, there was crap flying about once again. The players were allowed one free ticket and they could buy two. Reports came back that one of the committee had sold 20 tickets in a local pub and as a result the injured players weren't going as part of the official party. I was mindful that the non-playing squad members had not travelled when Wigan were at Wembley and we had been beaten.

As captain and spokesman, I had to go before the committee to argue their case, but got no joy. The only words were 'No, no, no'. I reported back to the players who asked me what we were going to do? At my forceful best, I replied: 'We are going to forget this crap, go to Wembley, win the Cup, enjoy the celebrations and then I will be jacking in'. Vinty beat me to it and he sent me a nice note to the effect that he thought he had taken the club as far as he could. True to form, I did jack it in and finished with Widnes after the Wembley celebrations.

Training moves

It's widely believed that pre-planned training moves are a new development, but there were moves at training sessions in those days, and at some times they had too many. I remember that coach Peter Fox called me into the England squad and I learned they had 27 moves. I said: 'I can't remember 27 moves in one training session Peter.' He told me to just follow Les Gorley. I said: 'We're having a new move, give me the ball and we'll create some gaps'. The game is very simple, it's about creating space and running the right lines. Some moves work but great players have great skills.

I've heard people say of violent play that what happens on the pitch stays on the pitch, but it doesn't always turn out that way. In an England versus Wales game, my club teammate Jim Mills was playing for Wales. One of the England forwards, who was a big fellow, kneed Tommy Cunningham, the Welsh hooker at the first scrum and split his nose. You could actually see the bone. Mills whacked the England forward, who should have got sent off, but wasn't. After the final whistle the England forward said to Mills: 'Good game Jim' and Jim flattened him again. The function after the match was at Jim's nightclub. The England forward was there and said to me that he was going to go over to Jim and apologise because the game was over. I told him that it wasn't a good idea - Jim had not cooled down yet and he should go home. He didn't take my advice, but fortunately Jim just told him to go away. At the end of the day though, we all respected the game and didn't want to harm its reputation. We were all honoured to play Rugby League.

Frank Myler took over as Widnes coach when Vinty left in 1975. I had played with him when he was the captain on the 1970 Ashes tour. He was the one who recommended me to Vinty at Widnes when I was on the list at Wigan for £6,000.

Following the problems leading up to Wembley, I had not played since the Challenge Cup Final. Around Christmas 1975, I was going to leave Widnes following Vinty's resignation, because I thought a few things had gone on. Frank came to see me. I was going to go to Oldham to be player-coach. Frank asked if I wanted to go there and I replied: 'You know me, if I had wanted to be there I would be there by now so get me out of it'. That is what he did. Oldham were going to give me £6,000, so Frank asked me how much would it cost to get me to stay and I said: 'How does one pound fifty sound?' He offered me a grand and I said if they had it to offer that would be fine.

Frank had made Reggie Bowden captain and said that he was doing well so I said: 'Fine, leave him there'. I liked Reggie anyway plus I knew that nothing would change, because I would still be boss out on the pitch. I would never hear a bad word said about Reggie, I love him and think he's a top man.

Frank was another top man, but he found it difficult remembering people's names. When he announced the team in the dressing room he would point at you and say 'you're in' and 'him over there, he's playing'. Sometimes he would write notes on the inside of his fag packet which tickled me. You won't meet a nicer man than Frank Myler though as long as you live.

Leading the way with Widnes (top photo courtesy *Widnes Weekly News*)

42

6. Things change, I'm the boss

Frank Myler had succeeded Vinty which was a difficult job. All of the players thought the world of Vincent, but to Frank's credit he soon had the train back on the rails and was winning trophies straight away.

Frank asked me what I thought of Stuart Wright the Wigan wingman. I told him to snatch their hands off because he would improve the side as long as he didn't sit him next to me on the coach. Frank had bought wisely in addition to Stuart and was a good judge of a player. I became assistant coach to Frank and went to watch the Rugby Union player Glyn Shaw at Sale. He looked fit, big, quick and got around the park. As I was leaving the stand with about 10 minutes left, Smith, the England scrum-half, went through and Glyn flattened him, although he didn't do anything dirty. I thought 'We'll have him, if he can lay a few out we'll be alright'. He was a hard man.

Frank Myler took us to Wembley twice, but St Helens in 1976 and Leeds in 1977 put it over us. In May 1978, he called it a day and persuaded the club to give me a go as player-coach. I had the man management skills from my central heating business - I was employing 44 people at the time.

One example of these skills was my idea that instead of a man and a lad taking eight to 10 days to complete a heating installation, I thought five men and one lad would do it in one day. The first customer was a little apprehensive but I put it across that we would cover everything with dust sheets and instead of having the house in turmoil for more than a week it would be done, working and bricked up in just one day. At 2.00pm, I called over and was chatting to her in the hallway. She remarked that she felt invaded. Just then a leg appeared through the plaster board in the hallway ceiling. It seemed to be waving at us. 'Just a little setback' I said. It worked out in the end .

I called everyone into the dressing room before my first training session in charge and told them that a few things had changed. I told them they had a new boss: me, and that they shouldn't be expecting an easy ride. All the lads were great when I took over, I'd played and died with them and they respected that.

I have been asked if I ever coached a player who reminded me of myself. My answer was that there weren't as many as awkward as me.

The first thing I did as coach was to get a goalkicker. I didn't realise at that time that I had an eye for a player although I can watch anybody now and straight away tell you if he's going to be any good or not. If someone is going to be a special player I can tell. Years later, when I saw Jonathan

Davies play his first game for Wales I knew he was something special. The reason I think I am so adept at spotting talent is that I have been watching rugby since I was eight and all the information is in my computer on top of my shoulders. I went to watch Mick Burke who was playing Union for Waterloo. He only played 20 minutes and then he got stretchered off. As he was being carried past me I asked him if he could kick goals. He told me he could, so I asked him how good he was and he said he could kick them from anywhere. I told him not to bull me and asked him what his best position in Union was. He told me 'fly-half' and I instantly replied that in my opinion: 'You're too fat for number six in Rugby League'. I told him he would have to play either full-back or on the wing for me. I put him on the wing and we won four cups that season, all because we had a goalkicker. Earlier that year I knew we wouldn't be far off but knew we were lacking a goalkicker. If you haven't got a goalkicker you're going to struggle.

People used to try and tell me that Rugby Union was a soft game but that day I saw Mick Burke play for Waterloo, it was anything but soft. I thought they were kicking lumps out of one another. It might be a bit soft at the lower levels, but at the higher levels it isn't. It was a vicious game in those days. The Union hierarchy pretended it wasn't, claiming it was a game for gentlemen, which was a load of rubbish. They used to kick everything above grass.

Managing players

I soon learnt about managing players. With one, I had a problem that he was never fit. I remember we had a Challenge Cup game and he was nowhere to be seen. I sent someone up to his house to see what was happening and the message came back to me that he'd had a row with his wife and wasn't coming. I was told I shouldn't go to his house because it would upset me. I went, banged on the door and managed to get in. On the floor was my player with the biggest pizza I've ever seen in my life. I said to him: 'It's cup week, it's a big game, you're supposed to be in training'. I was going mad at him, trying to stamp on the pizza while he was desperately trying to save it. I told him to get in the car and said 'I've a good mind to sell you'.

He was one of two players who I didn't do my best with. They were both special talents but I felt that they always had an excuse for everything. The other one, Brian Hogan, had asthma and if he'd have told me that I'd have gone easy on him. He came to me one day and said 'you're on my back all the time'. I said 'it's because you're at the back all the time'. He said 'well I'll start at the front, but I'll still finish at the back'. He wouldn't tell me he had asthma because he thought I'd get rid of him. All I would have done was come up with a training programme for him. He was a very talented player and a tough man too.

The other problem player could have been great, but he was always overweight. He hated training and would do anything he could to get out of it. You have to put the work in to get something out though. I remember Vinty saying to me 'Leave him with me on the Isle of Man, I'll get him fit for you'. But the player left after two days, Vinty called him lazy amongst other things and said he simply wouldn't do anything. He could con his way out of anything. He had everything though: big, quick, great temperament in matches and a great footballer. He did enough to get by which is sad because if he'd have gone for it he would have been something extra special, even a legend.

Another player was a bit like me, a bit of a rebel. He would always go for a few pints in Widnes and I warned him that if he did it when I was coaching he would be in big trouble. The next thing I found he'd been drinking in Sutton. I said to him: 'You're still drinking'. He replied that it was outside the town and I said: 'I can live with that but if it comes back to me you're in trouble'.

People write to you saying: 'How can you pick so and so? He's always on the juice'. I warned him that it would get him one day but it never did.

Boss at Widnes

What made me stop being the rebel was that I had gone to the other side. All of a sudden from being one of the lads I was the boss at Widnes. I remember planning: how could I do things differently to improve the situation? I put things in my square. It seemed to me that the best area for improvement was wage negotiation. In those days (and it was the same wherever I played) the committee or board would meet on the Tuesday night and give the coach the proposed payments for the players for the next match so the players could be told them at Thursday night training. Mayhem resulted and in some cases the terms were only sorted an hour before kick off and for certain games the board would come in and offer extra money at half time if you were losing. I told the players and the board that I wanted to negotiate all the match terms for the coming season, both league and cups up to and including the final, before the season got underway and that at training sessions I wanted to concentrate on winning the next game not arguing over £5 which after tax and other deductions was about £3.

The chairman asked me as did the skipper which side I would be on, it was even remarked that I could not sit on the fence. I reiterated that I would be on the side of common sense while sticking to my belief that this was the only way to go. It took some doing to have all this agreed, but the time spent was worthwhile if I was to become a successful coach.

It just so happened that the chairman at Widnes, was Jack Woodward, a gentleman whose great love was Widnes RLFC. I remember when we won at Wembley, Jack was seriously ill, so I backed the open topped bus down his drive. There was also the time I was going to sign a player from a club and told Jack what I was planning to do. Now Jack never forgot anything and he said that he had been talking to the chairman of the club concerned about this player a year ago. I asked if he thought the player had any bottle and he replied 'Any bottle? He whistles when he's going out for the coal'. That tickled me so I told Jack I wouldn't be signing the player concerned and Jack said 'Well I wouldn't.' People forget that the chairman's job should be to help the players and coach, not put Beecher's Brook in front of the coach and say: 'If you get over that we might keep you another week'. There wasn't a board of directors at Widnes at that time, they had a committee and Jack was chairman simply because he loved the club, that's all he was in it for. He had been loyal to Frank Myler, who had been coach before, in fact I never heard Jack call anybody. He would do what he could to help you.

The season was underway and we went reasonably well, winning the Lancashire Cup, beating Workington 15-13 at Central Park in the final, then for some reason we had a nightmare of a game and got battered. I was expecting the bullet because I always think of the best scenario and worst scenario that can happen in any given situation.

After training on the Tuesday after the game, Jack told me not to shoot off because he wanted to speak to me. I thought: 'This is it, they're getting shut of me'. I went to speak to him and said: 'Look if I'm getting bad news I'd rather hear it straight off'. He said: 'It was a bad result and I've been thinking, what we should do is have a do'. I was astounded. 'Have a do? I'm ashamed, I'm devastated. I want to kill them, I want to lock them in a room and beat the hell out of them. After letting us down we're going to throw a do for them?' Jack argued: 'Let's get some sausage rolls for them, bring their wives and their kids.' He went on to tell me 'What you've got to realise is that you can't make a lot of changes because we don't have the money to bring a lot of players in, you've got to work with what you've got'. I said: 'Jack, you're a legend'. When I told the players about the do they just said: 'That's what Jack does anyway'. However, Reggie Bowden suggested that he didn't think I would let the do go ahead.

But I announced: 'The do's on lads' and Reggie said: 'What's up with you?' He was told bluntly and directly where to go.

So anyway we had this do and went on to win the four cups. I'd signed Mick Burke to do the goalkicking, but that hadn't been a lot of money, little more than an amateur Rugby League signing really. When you're struggling, you have to be careful that you don't drive the players lower and lower.

Winning and losing can both become habits. I never said anything to my team after a game, it would just be a case of 'well done' or 'hard luck'. I would wait until the team meeting when they got back to the club on the Monday or a Tuesday as it was before full-time professionalism and have my say then. You should never slag your players off in public but on the other hand you don't defend them when they've had a poor game because the rest of the team think you're crazy because they all know he's let the side down. All you say publicly is 'Maybe I picked the wrong team, I'll have to think differently next time'. When I was experiencing difficult times, I remember a saying that is attributed to the gentleman who founded the McDonald's hamburger chain. It goes something like this 'Nothing succeeds like persistence - it beats endeavour and entrepreneurial ability'. The legendary Liverpool FC manager Bill Shankley used to say in times of adversity: 'There is nothing that a couple of signings and a couple of wins won't put right, and in the bad times you should look for the good things'.

As a coach I always got on well with the media. I always thought they were a part of my team whether I wanted them or not. The board is also part of my team, the players are part of my team, the speccies are part of my team, the media is part of my team because without all of them it doesn't work. I've never turned down an interview to anybody. Whenever I've told a journalist something that I told them I didn't want printing, they've never put it in. I've always trusted them and they've all been good men. Courting the media is part of a coach's job. You can't have an attitude of 'I'm not talking to them' because it won't work. If you treat them right, they treat you right.

I thought I needed a big, strong forward and I spoke to Jim Mills and said: 'You've played with Les Gorley, I rate him, what do you think?' Jim replied: 'He's the best, let's get him'. So I rang him and Les said he wanted a grand to sign. Jim said he would come with me to the signing because he was a mate of Les's. I asked Jim whether Les would want the grand and was told that he would. So I went to work and took a grand out of my own safe because I couldn't get a Widnes committee meeting organised in time. I signed him and gave him the grand. I had no receipt or anything and the committee said to me: 'How do we know you gave him the grand?' I said: 'If you don't know me by now, you've never really known me at all, keep the grand'. Anyway, they gave it me. He was a belting signing, just what we needed at the time and a hell of a man. His brother Peter was good too.

We went up to Cumbria to see Les after he finished playing, we filled a minibus. We said to Peter: 'Just get him in the pub and don't tell him we're coming'. We got there and Les said: 'What are you doing here?' We told him we had come to see him and he dashed off. We thought: 'We've come all this way and he's gone'. What he'd done was gone home to put his kids up somewhere else, cancelled our hotel so we could stay with him. That is the sort of fellow he is.

The Australians

The best game I ever played in my life came a few years later against the Australians for Widnes on 25 October 1978. We beat the Australian touring team 11-10 in front of a 12,232 crowd. I was on fire that night. They didn't put their best side out that night, they didn't pick powerful prop Les Boyd and I thought they might not be tough enough to take us on. We gave them a bit of stick and they didn't quite like it. I was man-of-the-match that night. I really enjoyed that game and I think the supporters did too. There's nothing quite like beating the Australians, especially as part of a club side. That night remains the last time a club side has beaten the Kangaroos.

The opposite side of the coin though was when they made me captain of the 1979 British Lions tourists which felt the full force of the Australian power and I was sent home injured. I suppose when one looks back, captaining a touring team at the age of 35 against the strongest Rugby League nation in the world was a bit of a cheek.

As Widnes player-coach in 1979, I was named Man of Steel. I also won Coach of the Year. That had never been done before and has never been repeated. It was good being player-coach because you were actually out there on the pitch with the players, telling them what to do and you could affect things more. As for the success, you get blasé, you think it's going to go on forever and it never does. Expectations went through the roof, the Widnes fans thought we were going to win everything.

My last game of Rugby League was the first game of the 1979-80 season at Leigh. I remember thinking 'I'm here on the pitch and I should be sitting on the bench over there'. If I hadn't have gone on the Great Britain tour I'd have probably played out the full season for Widnes.

I shouldn't have gone, my knee started swelling up again during that tour and it was the end for my playing career. Actually, I was going to jack in the game a few years earlier, but I remember talking to Bobby Charlton once and he said he could have carried on for a few more years, but had retired too early. Once you've retired you can't suddenly start playing again. At this point though, my enthusiasm for playing the game had gone, I wasn't prepared to put the training in anymore. I knew my time had come to finish playing and concentrate solely on coaching.

So that ended my playing career of what I called the game of snakes and ladders. Every time I was injured I looked upon it as 'hitting the snake' again with the knowledge that there were still 'ladders' to climb. I had quite a few injuries, not counting the damaged ligaments and sprains, here's the list:

- Broken kneecap which had a screw put in and taken out, leaving me up to my waist in plaster and out for almost a year;
- Four stitches to my left eye;
- Broken nose;
- Broken jaw;
- Loss of four teeth in three separate incidents;
- Two stitches to my top lip;
- Three stitches in my chin;
- Broken shoulder;
- Right arm bicep muscle was detached on one side;
- Broken ribs;
- Broken thumb;
- Dislocated fingers.
- Internal bleeding in my kneecap meant having another operation, shaving the bone on the inside of the kneecap;
- Broken big toe;
- Haematoma, but because some clown rubbed it, it meant bone calcified in the muscle.

In July 1980, when Reggie Bowden was leaving to go to Fulham he came to my house and said: 'Don't stand in my way'. I told him I already knew about the Fulham move which was supposed to be top secret. He said the club would get £25,000 for him and he promised that he wouldn't come back to Widnes to sign all my best players. I said that we had a deal, I would have taken £18,000 and let him go on his way, but if that's what they wanted to pay I thought I'd let them. He would later sign some players I wanted to get rid of at Widnes. I had lost some good players and when Great Britain international centre Malcolm Aspey looked like departing it was one too many as far as I was concerned. We were getting a bit weak.

I came home one day around this time and my wife told me that Syd Hynes, the Leeds coach had telephoned. I thought: 'Oh no, another coach wants one of my players'. So I rang him and asked him who he wanted to buy. He said: 'No it's not that, I want to sell Eddie Cunningham'. I replied that I thought Cunningham was trouble and I didn't want any trouble at the club. Syd said that I could have him for £20,000 and I told him that I didn't think we even had eight grand. He told me that he would let me sleep on it and then told me to call him in the morning. I put the phone down and shouted: 'Wahey'. We travelled to Leeds with two cheques because Jack Woodward had agreed a fee for Cunningham, an experienced Great Britain centre, with their chairman for £25,000. He said: 'Don't let me down' and I informed him that I had struck a deal for £20,000 to buy Cunningham and that was what we were paying.

I got £16,000 for Aspey, I couldn't wait to see him. He had had me like a puppet on a string continually saying: 'If you give me a bit more I might stay'. I told him: 'Malcolm, a deal is a deal'. I'll never pay more than what I have said to a player. I said to Aspey: 'This is my final offer, if you're going, you're going, if you're staying, you're staying, but you're not getting a penny more'.

I went to meet Malcolm, we couldn't meet in the office at Widnes, bearing in mind that the office was where the tumble dryer was. You'd be in a meeting and someone would come in and put the dryer on, drowning out whatever you were saying. So we met in The Crown pub and I couldn't wait for it, I'd been to Leeds and done the Cunningham deal for £20,000. I'd kept Jack's honour in doing the deal and also kept £5,000 for the club. I went in the pub and said: 'Malcolm, before you say anything, I've just agreed terms with Leeds for Eddie Cunningham, he's signed, everything is done and dusted.' He said: 'I might as well go'. I simply said 'God bless you'.

I'd got Cunningham for £4,000 effectively and he was twice the player as Aspey in my opinion, even though Aspey was a good player, he was now over 30 years old and past his peak. Eddie was magic, Wigan used to perform a move from a tap penalty where they would put three forwards with their backs to the opposition and pass the ball along. I told Eddie that if they did it against us he was to scatter them. He did that to great effect. I think his younger brother Keiron is great today, but he plays in the middle where perhaps he doesn't get as much trouble as Eddie did out wide.

Eddie was a flying machine and got more rough stuff than Keiron because when you're a flier everyone is after you but Eddie would take them on. Keiron does too. Eddie was a kid at Wigan when I was there and he played in the poor side we put out that managed to beat Saints 22-11 at Knowsley Road in the BBC2 Floodlit Trophy in 1967. He was one of the two best players that day. I thought that day he was special and he was.

In the early 1980s I was after a winger and someone told me about Ray Mordt who was playing in Zimbabwe. The board sent me over with this fellow who spoke Afrikaans. I took Wigan's last three annual financial reports with me because I knew they were also interested in him and I wanted him to see their financial position. I heard two of their directors were going out to talk to Mordt: Maurice Lindsay and Jack Robinson. We were going to a game and I saw them trying to hide behind a lamppost. I told my companion, who was from Wigan and had recognised them to go over to them and invite them to our hotel for a beer because there was no point hiding. I told them that they might as well go over Victoria Falls. They asked me what I meant and I explained that I had their last three balance sheets, had been to see Mordt and had showed him what Wigan could afford to pay him and what we could afford.

This was back in the days where Widnes paid their players more than Wigan because we were having more success. I told them they were out of the square already. They decided to give it one more go with him which I said they were entitled to do. Mordt then started saying he wanted copies of his contract for his uncle to look at, as well as his Aunt Mary and so on. I went to my hotel to do five copies of his contract to distribute around his family. I waited for him to phone me back. When he did he said he wasn't sure and I said in that case he shouldn't come. At the end of the day if a player is not fully committed to coming it's not worth chasing him. He actually signed for Wigan some years later and in my opinion he wasn't the success he would have been if he had signed for Widnes at that time.

I don't think it's a coincidence that so many players made it at Widnes at that time, I think it's a product of the environment we had there. New players were accepted at Widnes because the first team were all good players and weren't frightened of anyone else coming in. They just thought: 'You're going to have to be good if you're going to take my shirt and if you do take my place I know I'm good enough to go somewhere else.' That's how good players think. Bad players ask 'What are you signing him for?'

We had a good scouting set up at Widnes, it was well organised and that allowed me to bring the young players through. We weren't just bringing through kids from Widnes but the young talent from Wigan as well such as Lydon and Gregory. Like anything though, if you do something that is successful, people start copying you.

Andy Gregory

I went to watch a Widnes lad called Ashton play against Wigan St Patricks on a field near home. I used to go and watch the amateur sides play before our game on the Sunday even if I had a big game that day. In all my life, I never saw another coach there looking for talent. I would watch rugby anywhere and would always be out watching games. Ashton was up against a scrum-half by the name of Andy Gregory. I'd actually met Gregory about three years previously in Wigan. He'd given me a piece of paper noting how much money he would want to sign and I thought it was too high. I asked him after I'd seen him play against Ashton if he still had the piece of paper. He said he did. He also said: 'The money's gone up'. He had played a fantastic game so I signed him. Greg could throw balls as a kid that it had taken me years to learn.

I signed him in 1981, and thought that he was a little upstart so I kept him down for as long as I could. I thought he was like one of those balloons you have on a string. As soon as you let go he's gone. He was a great signing even though my initial impression of him was that he was a little fatty. I remember when I signed David Hulme, Greg wanted to know why. I just told him: 'He's fit, you're not'. It later came back to me that Greg started flying in training which I thought was good. Greg would have been great whatever happened, but I honestly believe that getting on his back made him greater than he would have been. It made him fit, quick and he put on about six yards in one close season; it was unreal. He had the skill but at first I thought he wasn't working hard enough, once I got him doing that, there was no stopping him. David Hulme would work his tripe off, but never had the skill of Greg. David was a tough lad, great kid, but never had the skill of Greg although he worked 10 times harder. So if you got Greg working as hard as David Hulme, you've got a great player and we did have.

I signed Joe Lydon in August 1982 following which his mam tried to give me the money back because another club were suddenly interested. I'd got him a place at Chester University through a friend of mine. His mam told me that he wanted to play Rugby Union. I said: 'No worries Mrs Lydon, keep the £6,000 we've given you, I'll not stand in his way of playing Rugby Union, as long as he knows that if he happens to play Rugby League he plays for me'. Whether another club was involved in this I don't know, but there was a smell of stinking fish. I thought he was another great signing, we got him for £6,000 and he was later sold for £100,000. That's not a bad profit but had I been doing the business I would have sold three others and kept Joe.

I coached Lancashire in the 1982-83 season. I'm good at a one-off job like this. If it's a one-off I can go and get a result. Lancashire were doing very poorly at the time, that's why they gave me the job. I thought I needed to get a nucleus together and try to get them playing together. Once I'd done that I thought that for the next four or five years Lancashire could go on and beat Yorkshire because the Yorkshire side had a nucleus of players. The Lancashire team was always changing because they were always getting beat. That never made sense to me. If my team got beat I didn't make 13 changes because what you're saying then is that you picked the wrong side in the first place. It didn't work out and I just thought this is not for me.

I was never asked to coach Great Britain. I wouldn't have done it anyway. Being honest, I think we'll find it very difficult to beat the Aussies again. They were paying their players proper money 20 years before we were and producing very talented youngsters by doing the job right.

Moving on

I remember Maurice Lindsay coming to my house in 1982 and offering me £35,000 if I would go and coach Wigan. I turned him down and my wife called me crazy. I was on £50 a week at Widnes in those days. At the time though, I didn't need the money and I told Lindsay that if he still wanted me the year after I would coach them then. I felt I would be due a change of scenery by then, but couldn't leave straight away because I had signed a lot of players for Widnes and told them that I would be working with them. I couldn't really leave them at that time. Three or four days later Lindsay rang me up to say they had recruited Alex Murphy instead.

I thought I had made a mistake not going to Wigan, then the people who had persuaded me to stay at Widnes informed me that they were all leaving the club. I thought bugger it and left the club in March 1983. I never know why I leave places; it's never just one thing. There's always something that sends me over the edge but there's a lot of stuff that has happened to lead to that point. One of the reasons I packed in though was because one of the directors came up to me and said: 'We could organise a benefit in your name which could make the club some money.' I thought that was a bit much.

Scoring for Widnes in the 1979 Lancashire Cup Final.
(Photo: *Widnes Weekly News*)

April 1979: An ankle injury against Huddersfield (Photo: Mike Brett)

7. Challenge Cup Finals with Widnes

Doug Laughton's record with Widnes, as a player, player-coach and coach is probably unequalled in modern Rugby League. Others may have won more honours as a player with one club, or as a coach, but it is hard to find anyone else who has won so much with one club, covering 18 years from 1973 to 1991.

This chapter concentrates on the 'great' occasions – the six Wembley Challenge Cup Finals. But as a player, Doug also had two Lancashire Cup wins, two losing finals in the John Player Trophy, and defeats in a Premiership Final and a BBC2 Floodlit Trophy Final.

As a coach at Widnes, Doug started his career with four trophies in a season. In 1978-79, when he was player-coach, as well as the Challenge Cup, Widnes won the Lancashire Cup, John Player Trophy (which became the Regal Trophy) and the BBC2 Floodlit Trophy. The next twelve years, in two spells at the club, apart from the Challenge Cup, Doug's teams won the Premiership five times, the Lancashire Cup twice and the Charity Shield three times. There were also final defeats in the Premiership, Lancashire Cup and two in the Regal Trophy. And as well as all the Cups, the club won the Division One title in 1977-78, and twice under Doug's coaching: 1987-88 and 1988-89.

But the game is about glory. And from the 1975 Challenge Cup Final victory against Warrington, to the 1982 defeat in a replay against Hull, Widnes were involved in six out of eight Challenge Cup Finals.

There were many pressures at Wembley Challenge Cup Finals. Doug remembers: 'Wembley always looks a bigger field than it actually is; whether that's because people are getting tired because of the nerves, tension or whatever, I'm not sure. Also, the Challenge Cup Final meant that players who were never interviewed on television were suddenly in front of the cameras.

It didn't bother me that much, I coped with it quite well, but that first time when you've never done it before is a bit of a tester. I remember going to be interviewed on the radio in Manchester. When I got to the studio there was nobody there to interview me. The guy producing the show pointed to where he wanted me to go. He mimed: 'We're on the air in five minutes, when the red light goes on, flick that switch'. There were hundreds of switches. I thought 'I'm a wireless engineer now, how bad is this?'

1975: Widnes 14 Warrington 7

Warrington came into this match as Cup holders. But it was a supremely fit Widnes team that proved triumphant, and reports of the match say that the final score did not do them justice. Widnes spent a week at Southport preparing for the final, training on turf similar to the Wembley pitch.

Widnes had reached the Final with three away wins: 13-4 at Swinton in the first round, then a 13-12 win at Hull, and a 10-4 victory at Oldham. In the semi-final, Wakefield Trinity were beaten 13-7 at Odsal.

Warrington took an early lead when Widnes did not clear a kick from Ashcroft near their line, allowing John Bevan to score. Whitehead converted. Ray Dutton kicked two penalties to bring the score to 5-4 to Warrington. Then on 33 minutes, Mal Aspey made a break on the left, passed to Eric Hughes who put Jim Mills in to score. Dutton converted, and scored another penalty before half time to give Widnes an 11-5 lead at the break.

In the second half, Whitehead scored a penalty after three minutes to make the score 11-7, but a penalty and drop-goal from Ray Dutton, who won the Lance Todd Trophy, secured the win for Widnes.

Coach Vince Karalius said after the game that "We murdered them. We were too fit and fast for them." It was Warrington coach Alex Murphy's first Wembley Challenge Cup Final defeat.

Jack Winstanley's report said that Widnes "owed their win to spectacular, flowing running and passing as much as to their vaunted defence." George Dowson wrote that Widnes's "superb pack, brilliantly led by skipper Douggie Laughton, trampled Warrington into the lush, green turf and, behind them, the backs ran riot at every opportunity."

Doug's mother Margaret was delighted with the victory. She had just retired from work, and asked her son to bring the Challenge Cup back to the town, as her uncle Paddy Douglas had done in 1930.

This final was the first one to have a schoolboy 'curtain-raiser'. Widnes beat Wigan 5-0 in an under-11 match. Joe Lydon played for Wigan, while Barry Dowd and David Hulme were in the Widnes team. All three later played for Widnes.

Doug remembers: 'I've got a tape of the Wembley final between Widnes and Warrington and my son asks me how I managed to play in it, it's that violent. Everyone was trying to knock each other's head off, you could hit people off the ball and there were no video replays to punish the offender.

That Widnes side had a lot of hard lads in it. Some of the sides I was involved with after that had greater stars and greater players, but they would have all struggled to have lived with that side because they would give you what for. I remember an opposition player saying once: "I hate going to Widnes, they're going to beat you and beat you up".

The highlight of my playing career was definitely lifting the cup in 1975, I'd lifted a lot of other cups before, but that was the realisation of a lifelong dream, lifting the famous Challenge Cup at Wembley Stadium. A lot of finals you won you just thought 'it's a cup, what's all the fuss about, we've won', it was no big deal. I mean I kept all my amateur stuff that I won, but I don't even know where half my professional stuff is. When I finally lifted the cup in 1975, it was like someone else yanked it in the air. When I see it on television now, I just think 'what a tosser'. I suppose winning the Grand Final is a great joy, but with Wembley, you had such a feeling of occasion, 86,363 people there, magic. I mean, the world-famous footballer Stanley Matthews played on that turf, all the great England football games there, just a tremendous place to be.

Every Wembley went quick, unless you were sat on the bench and then it seemed to last for about four days. When you were playing though, it seemed like you just had to click your fingers and it would be half time, the game just flew by. I enjoyed all the things surrounding the Challenge Cup final as well, it was fun. We trained at Southport for most of the week then travelled down to the hotel, the build up was all very enjoyable.'

Warrington: Whitehead, M. Philbin, Noonan, Reynolds, Bevan, Whittle, Gordon, Chisnall, Ashcroft, Wanbon, Conroy, Martyn, B. Philbin. Subs: Briggs, Nicholas.
Scorers: Try: Bevan. Goals: Whitehead (2).
Widnes: Dutton, Prescott, George, Aspey, Anderson, Hughes, Bowden, Mills, Elwell, Sheridan, Foran, Adams, Laughton. Subs: Karalius, Nelson – did not play.
Scorers: Try: Mills. Goals: Dutton (5). Drop-goal: Dutton.

1976: St Helens 20 Widnes 5

As Cup holders, Widnes went into this match as favourites. Widnes had already won the Lancashire Cup and the John Player Trophy, although Doug had missed both finals through injury. Some of the media had labelled St Helens 'the old men', but it was the experience of their team that saw them home.

To reach the Final, Widnes had beaten Batley 26-4, then had harder matches against Wigan – a 7-5 win, and a 6-0 win at Warrington. In the semi-final, Widnes beat Featherstone 15-9 at Swinton's Station Road ground.

The stadium was baking hot for the Final, which also seemed to favour the younger Widnes side. It was St Helens who opened the scoring. After 13 minutes, Eddie Cunningham scored; Geoff Pimblett converted for a 5-0 lead. A Pimblett drop-goal made the score 6-0 before two penalties from Dutton put Widnes back in the game, and made the half time score 6-4.

In the second half, a Keith Elwell drop-goal made the score 6-5, but that was as close as Widnes got. On 67 minutes, Pimblett scored another drop-goal to give Saints a 7-5 lead. A minute later, a try from Heaton, converted by Pimblett won the match for Saints, making their lead 12-5. Two further tries from substitute Peter Glyn, one converted, made the final score 20-5.

Jack Winstanley wrote that: "The dominance of the St Helens forwards – only Keith Elwell and Doug Laughton matched their fire, and even then only spasmodically – had the extra effect of drawing the sting from the Widnes halfbacks Reg Bowden and David Eckersley."

Saints' Geoff Pimblett won the Lance Todd Trophy.

Doug remembers: 'The Saints side were being called "old men" in the press. But they murdered us. Our front row were quite young and inexperienced. It was very hot and we couldn't breathe in the heat. I was very disappointed – I always wanted to beat my old clubs, especially at Wembley. Maybe we were complacent.'

St Helens: Pimblett, Jones, Cunningham, Noonan, Mathias, Benyon, Heaton, Mantle, Karalius, Coslett, Nicholls, Chisnall, Hull. Subs: Glynn, James.
Scorers: Tries: Cunningham, Heaton. Goals: Pimblett (3). Drop-goals: Pimblett (2).
Widnes: Dutton, Prescott, Hughes, George, Jenkins, Eckersley, Bowden, Nelson, Elwell, Wood, Foran, Adams, Laughton. Subs: O'Neill, Sheridan.
Scorers: Goals: Dutton (2). Drop-goal: Elwell.

1977: Leeds 16 Widnes 7

Widnes became the first team since Bradford Northern in the 1940s to reach three consecutive Wembley finals. Northern won two out of three. Widnes could not add to their 1975 victory, despite again starting the match as favourites. Around 20,000 Widnes supporters travelled south to the match, leaving the town as a ghost town as those who stayed behind watched the match on television.

Widnes had beaten Bradford Northern on the way to Wembley, a 19-5 win at Naughton Park following an 11-6 win at Bramley and 36-5 victory over Swinton. In the semi-final, Hull KR were beaten 14-5 at Headingley.

The final took place under a cloud. Two weeks before the match, Leeds young scrum-half Chris Sanderson had died in a league match at Salford. The match had been abandoned at half time, and had been traumatic for all involved.

His replacement, 19-year-old Kevin Dick, was playing his first Challenge Cup tie. But his lack of experience did not stop him scoring 10 of Leeds's 16 points, and being one the key players in their victory.

A penalty from Dick gave Leeds the lead after only two minutes. Leeds then had a try disallowed for a forward pass before Widnes equalled the scores after 11 minutes, Dutton kicking a 40-yard penalty.

Widnes then took the lead. Reg Bowden set up Mal Aspey who beat four Leeds defenders to score. Dutton converted to give Widnes a 7-2 lead. But after half an hour, John Holmes kicked through for Atkinson to score. Dick missed the conversion, so Widnes led 7-5 at half time.

Widnes started the second half on top, but could not turn their pressure into points. After 53 minutes, Leeds took the lead, with Dyl scoring. Seven minutes later, Kevin Dick scored a try, which he converted. This won the game for Leeds. Dick's drop-goal and penalty in the last three minutes finished a brilliant game for the young scrum-half who went on to have a long career with Leeds.

Leeds: Murrell, M. A. Smith, Hague, Dyl, Atkinson, Holmes, Dick, Harrison, Ward, Pitchford, Eccles, Cookson, Fearnley. Subs: D. Smith, Dickinson.
Scorers: Tries: Dyl, Atkinson, Dick. Goals: Dick (3). Drop-goal: Dick.
Widnes: Dutton, Wright, Aspey, Eckersley, O'Neill, Hughes, Bowden, Ramsey, Elwell, Mills, Dearden, Adams, Laughton. Subs: George, Foran.
Scorers: Try: Aspey. Goals: Dutton (2)

Doug remembers: Les Dyl played well for them, on the day they were the better side. Their backs had more pace then ours on the day.

1979: Widnes 12 Wakefield Trinity 3

In 1978, Leeds had retained the Cup, although it would be their last win until 1999. But in 1979, Widnes were back at Wembley, facing Wakefield Trinity, who were in their first Final since their defeat in the 1968 'watersplash' Final. This was Doug's first Challenge Cup campaign as player-coach.

The cup draw gave Widnes home matches in the first two rounds: a 12-5 victory over Workington followed by a 21-5 win over Wigan. In the third round, Widnes went to Fartown, and beat Huddersfield 14-0. The semi-final at Station Road saw Widnes reach Wembley again with a narrow 14-11 win over Bradford Northern.

This match marked the 50th anniversary of the first Wembley final in 1929, when Wigan had beaten Dewsbury 13-2. This was the first sponsored final: the State Express Challenge Cup. But the occasion and sponsorship did not have a positive influence on the match. It was remembered as one of the worst for many years. The first half was scoreless, the first time this had happened since 1956. It was dominated by defence and tough tackling. Wakefield played better, but their attack could not break down the well organised Widnes defence.

The forward battles continued after half time. On 49 minutes, Mick Burke gave Widnes the lead with a penalty. Then after an hour, winger Stuart Wright won the game for Widnes. Taking a pass from David Eckersley in his own half, he burst through the Wakefield defence, kicked to the corner and scored. Burke converted from the touchline and Widnes were 7-0 ahead. Four minutes later, Elwell put Widnes further ahead with a drop-goal.

Fletcher put Wakefield on the scoreboard with a try, but Smith missed the conversion. After 70 minutes, Eckersley scored a drop-goal to put Widnes 9-3 ahead, meaning that Wakefield needed to score twice to win the match. Instead, Hughes confused the Wakefield defence by lining up to kick a drop-goal, but instead sprinting for the line to score a try, and give Widnes the Cup with a 12-3 win. It was the club's fourth trophy in Doug's first season in charge.

Doug remembers: 'Prior to the Challenge Cup Final against Wakefield in 1979 someone in authority (who shall remain nameless) had expressed the opinion that I should remove the captaincy from Reggie Bowden as we had lost the last two under his leadership. I said: 'The thought has never crossed my mind'. Furthermore, Reg had played his heart out for the club, we had already lifted the Regal Trophy and the Lancashire Cup that season and I would be proud for him when he lifted the big one.

We went on to win the cup for the second time in 1979, beating Wakefield 12-3. It will probably be remembered as the most boring Wembley Challenge Cup Final ever. We had lost in 1976 and 1977, and I was determined that we would not lose again. I knew we could beat them if we shut the game down and that's what we did. It was boring but we got the cup. You sometimes feel you should go there and entertain but I couldn't stand the thought of going there and losing again. We just had to win that game.'

Widnes: Eckersley, Wright, Aspey, George, M. Burke, Hughes, Bowden, Mills, Elwell, Shaw, Adams, Dearden, Laughton. Subs: M. O'Neill, D. Hull.
Scorers: Tries: Wright, Hughes. Goals: Burke (2). Drop-goals: Eckersley, Elwell.
Wakefield Trinity: Sheard, Fletcher, Smith, Diamond, Juliff, Topliss, Lampkowski, J. Burke, McCurrie, Skerrett, Ashurst, Keith Rayne, Idle.
Scorers: Try: Fletcher.

1981: Widnes 18 Hull Kingston Rovers 9

In 1980, the Final had been a local affair – Hull Kingston Rovers beating Hull FC 10-5. But in 1981, Widnes were back at Wembley, facing the Challenge Cup holders again. At this time, the Humberside clubs were a leading force in the game. However, Widnes started the match as favourites. It was Doug's first Final solely as coach.

Nine of the team who had won the Cup in 1979 also played in this match for Widnes. However, in 1980, stalwart scrum-half Reg Bowden had left to become player-coach at Harold Genders' new club at Fulham. Mal Aspey and David Hull had joined him there. In the pack, Jim Mills, Alan Dearden and Doug had all retired. Making their debuts for Widnes in a Challenge Cup Final were 19-year- old scrum-half Andy Gregory, promoted from the 'A' team to take over from Bowden, Eddie Cunningham, who had scored for St Helens against Widnes in the 1976 Final, and in the pack Les Gorley, Brian Lockwood and Eric Prescott. Veteran Lockwood had won the Lance Todd Trophy for Hull KR the previous year and equalled Alex Murphy's record of four winners' medals with three different clubs. He had left Hull KR for Oldham, but then Widnes had signed him in a £30,000 deal. John Myler was on the bench for Widnes.

Widnes by now had become so frequent visitors to Wembley that a notice on the Runcorn-Widnes bridge before the final said: 'Welcome to Widnes – Twin Town Wembley'.

To reach the semi-final, Widnes faced three Yorkshire teams. Lowly Doncaster were vanquished 50-0 at Naughton Park in the first round, and then Castleford were beaten 7-5. In the third round, Widnes won 21-5 at Featherstone. The semi-final saw a local derby against Warrington at Central Park, which Widnes won 17-9. Warrington had taken an early 7-0 lead, but Widnes recovered to be 10-7 ahead at half time, and then dominated the second half.

61

Hull KR won the scrums in the first half 7-1, but continually wasted possession. Widnes's experience, combined with Gregory's prompting, saw them always ahead in the match. They took the lead after three minutes, when Mick Burke scored in the corner. Hull KR replied with a penalty three minutes later, but after 22 minutes, a penalty from Burke restored Widnes's three point lead. Then after 26 minutes, Lockwood passed to Burke who sent George in to score. Burke converted to out Widnes 10-2 ahead. A further Hull KR penalty and a drop goal for Widnes from Mick Adams made the half time score 11-4. Two minutes after the break, Andy Gregory scored a try on his Wembley debut. Burke converted, and then added a penalty to put Widnes 18-4 ahead. Burton scored a try for Hull KR, converted by Hubbard, but Widnes were never in danger of losing their lead.

Gregory's fine display was all the more remarkable as he had emergency dental treatment the night before the final. He came close to winning the Lance Todd Trophy on his debut, but the award went to full-back Mick Burke. Widnes's win put the club level with Wigan on six Challenge Cup wins.

Doug remembers: 'This was a special win. Half the team had gone to Fulham and we had to rebuild. Andy Gregory played despite having an abscess in his tooth. I felt he should have won the Lance Todd Trophy. I was made up for him – he had a great game.

This win gave me a lot of satisfaction – it was my team and my first win as coach. It is different as a player-coach as you are on the field. Lots of coaches and players never win at Wembley. You need a bit of luck sometimes, but we deserved our win.'

Hull KR: Hall, Hubbard, Smith, Hogan, Muscroft, Hartley, Harkin, Holdstock, Watkinson, Crooks, Lowe, Burton, Casey. Subs: Proctor, Millington.
Scorers: Try: Burton. Goals: Hubbard (3)
Widnes: Burke, Wright, George, Cunningham, Bentley, Hughes, Gregory, O'Neill, Elwell, Lockwood, Gorley, Prescott, Adams. Subs: Myler, Shaw.
Scorers: Tries: Burke, George, Gregory. Goals: Burke (4). Drop-goal: Adams.

1982: Hull 14 Widnes 14

Widnes returned to Wembley to face the other half of Humberside – Hull FC. Widnes's Challenge Cup run had started with a rare trip to Wales, to face League new boys Cardiff Dragons. A 19-8 win was followed by a trip to more familiar territory – Central Park. A 9-7 win was followed by another away draw – Bradford Northern at Odsal. An 8-8 draw was followed by a narrow 10-7 win in the replay. A three point win over Yorkshire opposition was repeated in the semi-final. Leeds were beaten 11-8 at Station Road. Leeds looked to be Wembley bound when near the end of the match, Adams lifted a huge kick towards the Leeds line. It bounced off the crossbar for Keiron O'Loughlin to score the winning try.

Hull had beaten Widnes 21-3 in the final league match of the season a week before the Final, but this match was much closer – Wembley's first draw since the dour 4-4 Halifax versus Warrington match in 1954.

Kieron O'Loughlin, John Basnett, Tony Myler and Steve O'Neill all made Wembley debuts for Widnes. Widnes took the lead with an Elwell drop-goal after four minutes, followed by a try by Cunningham which Burke converted for a 6-0 lead. But three penalties from Lloyd put Hull level at half time: 6-6. Eleven minutes into the second half, a Cunningham try put Widnes ahead, Gregory converting. Wright put Widnes 14-6 up ten minutes later. He intercepted Kemble's pass near the Widnes line, and ran 85 yards to score.

But Hull fought back. They changed tactics, moving the ball wide, and bringing Great Britain loose-forward Norton more into the game. He scored after 67 minutes; Lloyd converted to cut Widnes's lead to 14-11. With eight minutes left, 18 year old substitute Lee Crooks set up O'Hara to score. Lloyd missed the kick, and 14-14 meant a replay at Leeds United's Elland Road ground. Hull coach Arthur Bunting claimed that his team would have won if the game had gone on a little longer, but now the stage was set for a replay. Eddie Cunningham won the Lance Todd Trophy.

Hull FC: Kemble, O'Hara, Day, Evans, Prendiville, Topliss, Harkin, Skerrett, Wileman, Stone, Crane, Lloyd, Norton. Subs: Crooks.
Scorers: Tries: Norton, O'Hara. Goals: Lloyd (4)
Widnes: Burke, Wright, O'Loughlin, Cunningham, Basnett, Hughes, Gregory, O'Neill, Elwell, Lockwood, Gorley, Prescott, Adams. Subs: A. Myler, S. O'Neill.
Scorers: Tries: Cunningham (2), Wright. Goals: Burke, Gregory. Drop goal: Elwell.

1982 Replay: Hull 18 Widnes 9

Four days before this match, Widnes had beaten Hull 23-8 in the Premiership Final at Elland Road. Only 12,100 had attended that match, but for the Challenge Cup Final Replay, a capacity 41,171 crammed into Elland Road. Widnes fielded the same team as at Wembley. However, Hull made six changes. In the backs, veteran Humberside legend Clive Sullivan came in on the wing, and New Zealand international James Leuluai played at centre. In the pack, Lee Crooks came in at second-row.

Mick Burke gave Widnes an early lead. But after 33 minutes, Norton took a quick penalty, passed to Topliss who set up Kemble to score. Crooks converted, and Hull led 5-2. It was the first time in the final and the replay they had been ahead. Two minutes before half time, Topliss scored, giving Hull an 8-2 interval lead.

Widnes fought back after the break. A Burke penalty on 57 minutes made the score 8-4. Then a brilliant kick and run by Gregory set up Elwell, who passed to O'Loughlin who sent winger Wright in to score in the corner. Burke's conversion hit the post, so Widnes trailed by a point: 8-7. But then Topliss scored again for Hull, with Crooks converting to put Hull 13-7 ahead. Burke added another penalty to bring Widnes within four points of Hull, but then Crooks won the match for Hull, scoring a try with seven minutes left. His conversion made the final score 18-9 to Hull. It was revenge for David Topliss, who had captained Wakefield Trinity in their 1979 Final defeat to Widnes. He also won the man-of-the-match award. It was Hull's first Challenge Cup win for 68 years. Their last had been on the eve of the First World War in 1914 – a 6-0 win over Wakefield Trinity.

Hull FC: Kemble, Sullivan, Leuluai, Evans, Prendiville, Topliss, Dean, Tindall, Duke, Stone, Skerrett, Crooks, Norton. Subs: Crane.
Scorers: Tries: Topliss (2), Kemble, Crooks. Goals: Crooks (3)
Widnes: Burke, Wright, O'Loughlin, Cunningham, Basnett, Hughes, Gregory, O'Neill, Elwell, Lockwood, Gorley, Prescott, Adams.
Scorers: Try: Wright. Goals: Burke (3).

Doug remembers: 'We had played Hull in the Premiership Final at Headingley and battered them, so I didn't make any changes. They took the lead when David Topliss set up a try for them. Our team had looked great, but on the night we didn't perform. I had done everything I could. Sometimes as a coach there is nothing you can do.'

Widnes returned to Wembley in 1984, winning the Cup again against Wigan. But Doug had left the club in 1983. His next great triumph with Widnes was in 1989, winning the World Club Challenge against Canberra Raiders. This followed two consecutive Division One championships in 1987-88 and 1988-89.

Souvenirs of the 1975 Challenge Cup Final

THE RUGBY FOOTBALL LEAGUE
Patron :
HER MAJESTY THE QUEEN
President :
The Right Hon. THE EARL OF DERBY, M.C.

CHALLENGE CUP COMPETITION
FINAL TIE

WARRINGTON

v

WIDNES

on

SATURDAY, 10th MAY, 1975

KICK-OFF at 3.0 pm

at

THE EMPIRE STADIUM, WEMBLEY

PROGRAMME OF ARRANGEMENTS

D. S. OXLEY,
Secretary

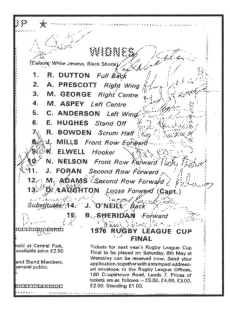

WIDNES

(Colours: White Jerseys, Black Shorts)

1. R. DUTTON   *Full Back*
2. A. PRESCOTT   *Right Wing*
3. M. GEORGE   *Right Centre*
4. M. ASPEY   *Left Centre*
5. C. ANDERSON   *Left Wing*
6. E. HUGHES   *Stand Off*
7. R. BOWDEN   *Scrum Half*
8. J. MILLS   *Front Row Forward*
9. K. ELWELL   *Hooker*
10. N. NELSON   *Front Row Forward*
11. J. FORAN   *Second Row Forward*
12. M. ADAMS   *Second Row Forward*
13. D. LAUGHTON   *Loose Forward* (Capt.)

Substitutes: 14. J. O'NEILL   *Back*
15. B. SHERIDAN   *Forward*

1976 RUGBY LEAGUE CUP FINAL

Held at Central Park, available price £2.50 and Stand Members, general public.

Tickets for next year's Rugby League Cup Final to be played on Saturday, 8th May at Wembley can be reserved now. Send your application, together with a stamped addressed envelope, to the Rugby League Offices, 180 Chapeltown Road, Leeds 7. Prices of tickets are as follows :- £5.00, £4.00, £3.00, £2.00. Standing £1.00.

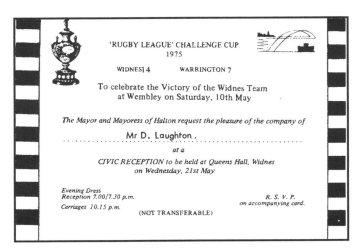

'RUGBY LEAGUE' CHALLENGE CUP
1975

WIDNES 14   WARRINGTON 7

To celebrate the Victory of the Widnes Team
at Wembley on Saturday, 10th May

The Mayor and Mayoress of Halton request the pleasure of the company of

Mr D. Laughton ,

at a

*CIVIC RECEPTION to be held at Queens Hall, Widnes
on Wednesday, 21st May*

Evening Dress
Reception 7.00/7.30 p.m.
Carriages 10.15 p.m.   (NOT TRANSFERABLE)

R. S. V. P.
on accompanying card.

Top left: The cover of the Rugby Football League's programme of arrangements.
Top right: The Widnes team line up in the programme, signed by the players
(Both courtesy the Rugby Football League)
Bottom: Invitation to Halton Council's Civic Reception

The 1975 and 1976 Finals

Top: 1975 The cup belongs to
Widnes – Doug with coach
Vince Karalius

Bottom: 1976: Going forward
against St Helens
(Photo: *Widnes Weekly News*)

The 1979 Final

Doug Laughton is tackled by Alan McCurrie and Bill Ashurst,
watched by Les Sheard. (Photo: *Widnes Weekly News*)

1982 Cup Final

Leading out Widnes at Wembley. The Widnes chairman is Jack Hayes.
(Photo: Aaron Agencies Studio)

Action from the replay at Elland Road:
Mick Burke taking a penalty for Widnes
(Photo: Aaron Agencies Studio)

8. Down the same road twice

I was out of the game for a couple of years before returning to Widnes in 1986. I just carried on with my central heating business in the meantime. A few clubs rang me in the first six to eight weeks after I left Widnes, but the phone soon starts going cold when you're out of the game. Approximately eight weeks before I returned to Widnes as coach I was talking to their present coach; and a mate of mine, Eric Hughes. He was under pressure to sell players for financial reasons.

Alex Murphy was coach of Saints at the time and they were desperate for forwards. I told Eric Hughes to sell one of his forwards to Saints because I knew that they would pay around £25,000 for one. I told him that if he didn't sell somebody of his choice, then the consequence would be that he would be the one to go. I told him to sell his worst players so he could keep his best.

Sure enough, the Widnes board sold Joe Lydon, one of my signings and a top player, for £100,000 to Wigan. As a result, Eric Hughes resigned. If he had sold two or three lesser players beforehand, though, he could have possibly kept the top players at the club. I was trying to help Eric at the time. The day after he packed in, someone from Widnes came round and knocked on my door. I was a bit fed up with the fact that Wigan were dominating the game at the time and just thought: 'Someone's going to have to stop that lot'. That was one of my reasons for getting back into coaching. If you had someone like Lydon playing for your club and he played really well against Wigan, they would just try and sign him. They had the biggest gates and the most money as a result. You couldn't compete with them on that level. Widnes just didn't have the money or the resources to continue the uphill fight against Wigan. That was the common thought at the time, although it was certainly not my opinion.

During my second spell at Widnes we managed to beat the all-conquering Wigan side to two league titles, in 1988 and 1989. It should have been three, but that season I thought that the fixtures changes did not help our cause. I remember one of the Widnes directors saying to me when I first came back as coach: 'What we want is to get Wigan in the cup draw and get a nice big gate'. I said: 'That won't do me, how about beating them?' I think I managed to find a hole in the net you might say. When I was a player at the club, you were on so much for a win and so much for a loss. Now that contracts were starting to come into the game, Wigan were paying people far more per season than we could afford.

Mind you, I recommended Franco Botica to Maurice Lindsay. He rang me and said: 'Have you seen anyone on this New Zealand Rugby Union tour? I know you'll have who you want by now.' I said: 'The only one I've seen is that reserve number 10. He's a good little player and he can kick goals'. He was Frano Botica and joined Wigan in 1990. A couple of years later when Martin Offiah scored 10 tries for Wigan against Leeds whom I was coaching at the time and Botica was 'back heeling' kicks from everywhere, I was thinking: 'what have I done here?' I had a goalkicker at Widnes at the time though and didn't need Botica. With him, tries weren't worth four points, they automatically became six.

I thought that Wigan were cornering the market, lads from amateur Rugby League were costing £6,000 to sign on and if a quality player from another League club became available Wigan would just outbid you. So I had this thought that there must be someone in Rugby Union that could do me a job. Martin Offiah was my first sortie and I know he won't mind me saying that his contract was £95,000 over 10 years. A committee member remarked that if he was a failure we were stuck with him for 10 years. You wish! I remember thinking about that man: 'I wonder how he learned to walk'. As well as the £95,000 there was winning and losing pay. The players we signed from Union could be employed outside Rugby League because it was not full time professional then.

You still had to sell League to the Union players of course, but I was a natural born salesman. When I came back from Australian club Canterbury, the person I had left looking after my business had just bought four new vans for the firm even though there was no work and we were really struggling. I went door-to-door looking for business in the Thatto Heath area of St Helens. One fellow recognised me and couldn't believe I was knocking on his door. His words irked me: 'Doug Laughton, rugby star, trying to flog me stuff on my doorstep'. I said: 'I'm here to save you money'. Before long, I had most of the street signed up.

Plastic pitch

When I went back to Widnes, Wigan were getting all the publicity and I needed to get our club in the papers and wondered how I might go about doing it. I thought 'we'll have a plastic pitch'. I went down to Queens Park Rangers FC to have a look at their pitch. So, the next thing, I've got a piece of plastic, not as big as my rug, outside the Widnes social club in the car park. The BBC came to film the story. I came out with all this stuff about how this new playing surface was going to revolutionise the game. I got our prop John Fieldhouse to run on it and told him to say that it was quite hard to get tackled on while Kurt Sorensen said that he thought it was alright. The morning of the press conference we were staging the

Rugby Football League said: 'We couldn't have a plastic pitch as it is against Rugby League bye-laws. I thought: 'Wahey, more fuel for the fire'. I responded by saying: 'They can't tell us what we can and can't play on, who do they think they are?' We had hundreds of people in the car park looking at this little strip of plastic. Talk about Barnum! All the national press were there.

I sometimes think I got distracted from my real job by all these other things I was doing but it was all part of the same job really. It gave the players a buzz to be in the papers.

Big Australian international Noel Cleal was at the club when I returned. He was obviously a great player but he couldn't work me out. He had a shoulder injury and I wouldn't play him until he had recovered. I heard him saying: 'Why wouldn't you pick your best player?' I said: 'You're not the best if you're injured'. I told him to have a couple of weeks off and get himself right. Like other Australians, he sometimes had problems with 'winter' Rugby League. I remember him playing at Featherstone in a blizzard, he wanted to go off at half time, his fingers were blue with cold.

As a coach there was only one referee I ever had problems with. He used to keep us further back than everybody else. I told him I had proof on video. Subsequently, he took charge of us in a semi-final and he kept the other side so far back. He asked me how that suited me and I told him that it didn't. He told me there was no pleasing me and I told him that I didn't want any advantage. I remember when we played Wigan once and the ref took me and Colin Tyrer for a chat. He told us: 'I think that if someone cracks you on the park, you should be able to crack them back'. That was all I needed to hear and instructed my players to murder Wigan on the park, and give them everything. We were a big, strong side. The likes of Emosi Koloto and Paul Moriarty got away with murder, we battered them that day. The ref was telling the Wigan players they could hit back and they were saying: 'We don't want to hit 'em back'. They weren't looking forward to playing us again after that game.

In 1988, we had already won the league when it was clear that it was between me and Alex Murphy at Saints for coach of the year and that the winner of Widnes versus St Helens in the Premiership final would get the award. I thought this rumour was a load of bull to be honest, but typical of some of the off the field things that seem to occur in our sport. In any event, we took Saints to the cleaners, winning 38-14, scoring seven tries. I did win the Coach of the Year award.

I always thought I spent more time on coaching than Alex. I spent loads of time reading all manner of books. I thought that the craziest book

I ever read was *Train your super mind*, which involved me having to oscillate with a lolly ice stick, a piece of string and a wooden bobbin over the carrots in Tesco. I had to give the book away, it was clearly sending me wacko. I even used to take players to hypnotists. I was well into the psychology of it all. I would use anything I could to be the best so long as it was legal. I took on board the things that were helpful and tried them.

I remember when the tackle count was first considered to be an important factor in the game I told my chairman that without looking at the figures I could tell him the top three and bottom three every week. I added that the top three were the ones I wanted to keep and the bottom three were the ones I wanted to lose as defenders. I also remember the same chairman brought in this fellow from Liverpool University who could measure fat content. I said: 'I'll do it for you instead' and gave the following judgments on players that, again, have been amended ever so slightly:

'Fat basket'.

'Almost fat basket'.

'A fit basket'.

The sports scientist then gave basically the same 'official' judgments, for example if he said you had 60 per cent fat you were a fat basket. Still I suppose it was keeping someone in a job. There are more jobs surrounding sport these days than I can believe. Mind you, it seems like there are also more people checking who's on the dole than there is actually on the dole. There is also so much jargon. I made players do '10 on the bike' at Widnes. This meant 10 non-stop sprints between the try line and the 25-yard line. They later called exactly the same exercise a bleep test.

Alan Tait

In 1988, I got a phone call from Ike Southward, and in a strong Cumbrian accent he asked: 'Have you seen this Tait boy playing centre for Scotland Rugby Union? He's magic'. So I went up to see him. His dad used to play for Workington and his dad said to me: 'It's an honour to see you Douggie' as if I was a legend or something. He told me his son was ready to come to League. When trying to sign him initially I spoke to his dad all the time until I said that it was Alan I wanted to sign and not him. So I went to talk to Alan and said 'What do you want?' He said '£8,500, not a penny more, not a penny less' which would have been fine when his dad had been playing, but not any more. I said to him: 'I'm going to pretend I never heard that'. Although I had a job to do for Widnes, the average first team player was earning about £18,000 a year. I didn't know if the lad was any good so I was hedging my bets. I said: '£8,500, total for a 10 year deal?' He said: 'That's alright, I'll get my match fees on top of that', but you got your match fees anyway. I told him that I couldn't seriously agree to this because he wouldn't be a happy player and I needed happy players. He said: 'All right then, how about £50,000 spread over 10 years?' I said: 'I'm happy at that' and he said: 'So we do a deal then?' and I said 'No, because you won't be happy with it'. I said: 'Look give me some figures, when it gets high I scratch my nose and when it gets low I rub my chin'. So we stood there rubbing our faces for about 10 minutes. Alan just said: 'I want to come, I want to play League'. I think he'd had enough of Rugby Union because you got rag all for playing Union then. He signed for Widnes in April 1988. And he was another player that Saints were interested in; but they always got there four weeks after me!

I ended up giving him £85,000 spread over 10 years, it was still £8,500 a year, amateur signings cost you £6,000. I just thought if it turns out he's no good we do a deal, pay him off and send him on his way. If it turns out that he's good, he's worth a lot of money - we sort out his contract correctly. Two years later Alan said to me: 'you conned me' I said: 'I didn't con you, if I'd conned you I would have signed you for £8,500 in total for a 10-year deal'. Taity and I had the rounds of the kitchen about it until he admitted that if I had let him he would have signed for just £8,500 as opposed to getting that same amount per year. So we did a few things for him like getting him a job at the ground and so on. He was quick, a good player, a good man and loyal, so we brought some of his contract payments forward.

I gave Taity 10 on the bike in his first training session and he nearly died. He gave me some bull that the sun shining in his eyes on the drive down had made him feel ill. I said 'Ok we'll see how you do at it next week then'. If people said to me: 'Bloody hell that was hard' then I'd go easy on them. If they came up with excuses they got it twice as hard. Further down the line, Taity did the best bleep test ever at the club just to get to me. You want the people who compete.

If Taity comes south these days he always calls to see me and you can get no better compliment in life than that. I felt that he was a right moaner though. He would moan about everything because he wanted everything to be right. They reckon Manchester United footballer Roy Keane is the same way. If you're doing a job as difficult as I was doing and someone is pointing out things to you, you think 'that's right', if he isn't right you explain to him why not. The more information you get, the better.

I originally signed Tait as centre but thought that with the game changing, and becoming faster, you needed someone coming from the back at pace. I thought it was the best attacking option. If someone like Taity gets a yard in front he scores. You would need someone as fast as Martin Offiah to catch him. I think defence is great but if you score 10 tries to their one you're going to win the game. I hated defence oriented Rugby League. I once lectured on defence at Swinton with all the first team coaches and Australians like Rod Reddy present and I thought 'What am I doing here?' I liked to attack. Let the ball do the work and get the ball to beat the man. I think the Aussies are now playing old-fashioned rugby, they let the ball do the work. Rugby League can be the most exciting game or the most boring game. It's a bit like draughts, if you get down the other end you score, if you're down your own end they score. No matter what you do to get there the end result is always the same. I helped bring the rule in where if you are held up over the line you get the feed at the scrum because you were trying to score.

I also brought up the 40-20 rule after remembering how Bill Ashurst kicked that way. Before that rule came in, a defence could line up fully, now they have to drop men back to prevent a touch kick, and there is more room and chance to attack. The more options you've got to attack, the better. That's the reason I like association football because you see goals.

It is now very rare that you could get the sort of result in Rugby League that you could in association football where it is possible that a lower division side could beat a Premiership side.

9. A rugby player from London

Ray French rang me one day and said: 'Douggie, my lad played Rugby Union for Liverpool St Helens against this fellow from Rosslyn Park a few weeks ago and this guy ran rings around him, he couldn't even tick him, he's special, his name is Martin Offiah. I told Saints to look at him but they sent someone and aren't interested'. I believe that the actual words that came back from Saints about Offiah were 'uncoordinated clown'. I felt that Saints were bad at scouting players in those days, but they have got it better now. I went to watch Offiah at Orrell and he didn't do a lot. Then I watched him on BBC television's *Rugby Special* which was featuring the Middlesex Sevens competition he was playing in. A player broke through who I knew was of Olympic standard over 200 metres, yet Offiah turned round and caught him. I thought 'This lad is quick, I'm on the road to sign him'.

So I sent my chief scout, Eddie McDonald to get in touch with him and we went down to meet him in London. I infamously spilt half a lager over his yellow pants. Martin said in his book that Eddie did it, but it was me who knocked it over. He was only about 20 at the time, but was over six foot tall and obviously fit. When you went signing players, you were sussing them out. I had to see whether they would fit in with the rest of my boys, whether they had the same sort of beliefs. I'm not talking religious beliefs.

I went down to London again and asked him if he was still interested and he said he would have to talk to his mam. So we went down to London for a third time and I said: 'I need to get the money from the committee to sign you, so you need to give me some idea of what sort of money you are looking at'.

He gave me a figure and I went down again, this time on a Friday dinnertime but he just changed the goalposts a little bit. I had the contract sorted out to the figure he had asked for prior to this change, so I rang my secretary and told her to get on a train to London from Runcorn because I needed her to type up the new version. I asked her to get the club to provide her with some forms to bring with her. I asked Martin to join us for dinner that night because I knew that men trust women better than they trust other men. I don't know why, but they do.

I really wanted to get the deal done, I don't know why, but I had a very strong feeling that this lad was very special. I thought: 'He's a nice man, he's a gentleman, he speaks well to ladies, he says 'please' and 'thank you', what a good man he is'. I said to him: 'I'll play a game with you, it's called "Tell the truth", you ask me three questions and I'll tell you the truth on all three as long as I can have my three back'. We shook on that. We played and one of my questions was: 'I've got one problem: I've got a team to run. We're in the middle of a season and I can't keep coming down here courting you, as much as I like you and think you're a nice guy. I'm going to need a decision soon'. He replied: 'Well I can't make one tonight' and I said: 'Well if you can't, you can't.' He said that he might be able to give me a decision tomorrow.

I got up the next morning like a caged animal as I still hadn't got the deal signed. I told my secretary: 'I'm going to walk round the park, I want you to ring him up and play "Tell the truth" with him. I want you to tell him this too: that if he doesn't sign by one o'clock today I will never come back. You know what I'm like, what I say I mean'. I came back from my walk and thought: 'I've made a mistake with this kid, I shouldn't have been so aggressive', but I couldn't spend any more time on it because I had a business to run and a club to coach. When I came back my secretary was at the typewriter. I asked her what she was doing. She told me she was typing up Martin's contract and that it was exactly what we had agreed on last night. I asked her what she had told him and she replied: 'The truth'. I said 'Well let's have it then' and she replied: 'Well there's nothing much to tell really'. I said: 'I want to know'. She told me that he had asked could he trust me and she replied that he could trust me with his life.

He came to sign and I said: 'I want you to see a solicitor first', but he said: 'I don't need one'. I replied: 'We'll pay for it'. He said: 'No, I asked my mum and she asked me if I trusted you. I told her that I did and she said in that case I didn't need a solicitor.' I told him I would never let him down and I never did. He never let me down either. That was rock solid. I trusted him, he trusted me and nothing has happened since to change that.

Once we agreed the deal, I was told by the club that they had second thoughts and the money wouldn't be provided because they weren't prepared to 'back my whims'. I said: 'That's OK, Maurice Lindsay will come up with the money for him and Wigan will take him on'. That remark seemed to concentrate a few minds because very quickly it was 'all hands in favour' and the deal was well and truly back on. We had paid him £10,000, and you would pay an amateur Rugby League kid £6,000.

He told me his name was pronounced Offyer and I warned him then and there that he would be called 'Chariots Offiah', from the film *Chariots of Fire*. Widnes people will pronounce it 'O-fire' and then you're bound to get chariots stuck in front of it, I told him. I didn't come up with the slogan, but he got stuck with it anyway. I don't suppose it did him any harm.

When he came to his first training session with us I told him: 'Show me, be the man' and he raced down to the try line before the other players had got going. I just thought: 'Yes, what a star, we'll get Wigan nilled; we've got a try scorer'. It was like discovering the Rock of Gibraltar, Galileo, Nijinsky, you name it, I've got it here with this one. He flew and I thought: 'I must have a player who can put this kid in the clear surely'. He was big for a winger, lightning fast, the sidestep on him was unreal, someone labelled him a freak, he wasn't a freak but he was special. Colin Tyrer, my assistant coach, would say: 'You can't expect Martin to score all the time', but that is exactly what he did. If there was a game where he hadn't scored yet you knew you weren't far from the moment when he would burn away the opposition and score a try, he was like lightning.

In his first game his defence was brilliant. He could chase a player from one side of the field, running round all the others, and then catch the player he was after. Wigan later said they made him a better player, but no-one ever made Martin Offiah a better player, he was born a great player. He listened to everybody, took the good things on board, threw the rubbish out and got on with being a great player of his own vocation. I didn't make him great, he was great the day he walked through the gates of Widnes Rugby League Club.

A gentleman

He was a nice lad, a gentleman, what he said he meant, he kept his word, my wife loved him, and for all those reasons he became part of the family when he moved up to Widnes. All the same, I had a few run-ins with him like you do with any great player. It was my wedding anniversary and I'd had a committee meeting following which I was going to the Black Horse for a meal with my wife. I get there to be told that Martin wanted to see me because one of the players had been calling him a 'black bastard'. He'd only been there a few months at this point. He told me that he was off and would never play for Widnes again. I said: 'That's charming, we've got a 10-year deal here and you're going to throw it away. What do they call me Martin? What do they say about me?' He said 'You know'. I said 'I do know but you tell me'.

I asked him: 'Do they call me that grey-haired old bastard?' and Martin started laughing. I said: 'I can't help the grey hair but I could probably dye it black because I think black is a better colour than grey don't you? You're either annoyed at being a bastard or a black man.' He said: 'I'm not ashamed of being black'. 'Nor should you be' I told him before going on to tell him to get back in there, tell his tormentor where to go and fight for himself. I then told him not to mither me on my wedding anniversary again. My wife said: 'You were a bit strong on him there' but I pointed out that he was only a kid and he would learn. I had the player who had been calling him into my office and told him that if he ever called Martin that again he would be out of the building and also that Martin wasn't a bastard as he had a mother and father.

Try celebrations

People always talk about Martin's exuberant try celebrations. My view on it was that if he did something that I felt was against the spirit of my game I would ask him if we really needed it, I didn't rollick him though. You have to remember that there were instances of people throwing bananas on the pitch at him which really annoyed me. The next time he scored after this happened he jumped on the wall surrounding the pitch and there were complaints. I told them where to go because if people could throw bananas at him I thought he should be allowed to celebrate any way he wanted. He could have picked the bananas up and thrown them back. However, he was above that.

I was lucky that even though there was the Catholic versus Protestants, Labour versus Tories intolerance around when I was a kid, my mam and dad both believed that people were the colour they were because of where they lived on the planet and how life evolved. My wife's mam and dad thought the same. We never thought that people with different coloured skin were inferior to us. My grandmother used to say: 'There's nobody better than you and there's nobody worse'. The 'nobody worse' bit would prompt me to ask: 'Am I that bad?' I was taught to treat people with respect. We were raised that way even if we never had a great education.

Martin moved in with us at one point with us because he was ill. My God, I thought I'd never get rid of him! I kept on telling him to get out of bed and he would reply that he was sick. 'Sick? Sick? You should be dead you've been here so long' came my reply. I had to empty his sick bucket and remonstrated with Martin that he should go to the toilet should he need to be sick. I don't think he'd been mothered for a while because it's a big thing moving up from London and leaving your mum and everything.

Martin did not get special treatment from me; he got treated like all the rest. I know he has said I treated him well, that's because he's one of the honest ones. That's because he made it, the ones who didn't, say: 'Doug was terrible with me'. You don't pick your worst team though do you? 'Why am I not getting picked?' I was often asked. 'It's probably down to the fact that you're useless' I replied.

Martin hadn't scored on his debut against Halifax and I told him at half time in the following Lancashire Cup match at Runcorn that you can't buy a try-scoring winger who doesn't score tries and gave him a little pat. He got off the mark in the second half and was well and truly up and running. After this it became a bit of a superstition for him, where he would hang about near me in the dressing room until I gave him a bit of a rub. I gave Tommy Martyn a rub at a wedding a couple of years ago, because he told me he kept getting bad injuries and he's not had as many since. He wanted another one but I told him it might take the first one off! I gave him a bit of advice also telling him not to go in so hard all the time and hang back a bit, make the forwards do your tackling.

People ask me what Martin was like if he didn't score in a game, I tell them he was the same as me: upset. It didn't happen that often anyway so I ask them which game they are recalling. He thought scoring tries was his job so would be on a downer if he hadn't scored. I remember David Hull crossed the line in a John Player Final and he didn't put the ball down immediately. Everyone was screaming 'put the ball down'. I don't think he could believe he'd scored. Martin could have been on his own line and thought he could score while others could be a foot from the try line and still didn't think they couldn't score because they have this mindset of 'I never score'.

During one game Martin said to me 'I'm not getting the ball, I want to play on the other wing' so I switched him although I did warn him that he was better on his normal wing. At half time he came in and said 'It's awful, switch me back'. Martin had got no ball in that half because all the players used to pass to their left. And he'd moved to the right. But when he had Gene Miles as his centre partner at Wigan he proved what a great winger he was. If I'd had have had Gene Miles with him at Widnes he would have scored more tries than anybody ever. Martin is certainly the best winger of the modern era and there will always be comparisons between him, Billy Boston, Tom van Vollenhoven and Brian Bevan. Do the comparisons really matter? I'd settle for any two from four.

Training

When we played tick and pass in training Martin would always be on the side of me and Colin Tyrer. No-one could even tick Martin. If anyone complained about the choice of sides I would inform them that I had the brains and Martin had the legs. Colin's legs had gone by this point. We always won, no one could get near Martin. 'You're not having Martin again', 'oh yes we are' at every game. If they continued complaining I would offer them Tyrer, but I still had Offiah. Kurt Sorensen would be captain of the other side and would say he wasn't going to play but I explained that Martin was new to the game and I had to teach him! On other occasions I would let Kurt be one captain and Martin the other and Martin would always pick me first anyway! He was so much fun as well. You're probably more fun when you're young, but I think the happiest time of Martin's life was at Widnes because we were all idiots. We had a laugh. People should laugh more; at the end of the day it's nice to be nice. We used to take the mickey out of each other all the time. If you had a new joke you had to leave it till you got in the bath because if you told it on the training pitch it would have been passed round within seconds. That was a special time, it was fun.

On 16 April 1989, we beat Wigan 32-18 at Naughton Park in front of 17,323 fans to win the title. Martin got a hat-trick, and that day will always stay in my memory. It's the day he scored his best try for me. It was his third - he went round Steve Hampson as if he wasn't there, after going through half the team. He scored that many I can't remember some, but with that one helping us win the league, it was a big one.

When he told me he wanted to leave, I told him that we had a deal and that I had kept my side of it and he should keep his so it wasn't a matter for discussion. At the end of the day though, I had been talking to Leeds about coaching there. I'll tell you this, if I'd have stayed at Widnes, I am almost sure Martin would have, of course it would have cost us more, not as much as the king's ransom I felt that Wigan lashed out. One of the reasons I went to Leeds was because I thought I would get more money to spend on players, I got some but not as much as I thought I would have done. It wasn't a mistake going there though because I was well paid and started my second pension which seemed a good idea at the time.

Was Martin induced to leave Widnes? It's like that song: 'I've often walked down this street before but the pavement always stayed beneath my feet before'. What I do know is that if I go to that same girl on that same street at the same time, it's not a coincidence, I've made that happen. I don't believe in coincidences.

I didn't tell Martin I was leaving for Leeds because it was my own business. When he told me he would never play for Widnes again, he never told me he was going to Wigan. I knew anyway as who else could afford him? It took a while to sort out, and as I warned him 'It's going to be painful Martin, Widnes will want to hang onto you'. I wouldn't have hurt him the way Widnes did. I would have let him go if he had wanted to go that much. I don't believe in putting people out of the game.

Martin gave me his last Widnes shirt after the Premiership Final against Hull in 1991, which we lost 14-4. He was close to my family; he came to our house at Christmas when he moved up to Widnes because he had nowhere else to go. His family was in London and we played on Boxing Day so he had to be in Widnes. He's my mate; he's never done anything to make me think otherwise. He never knifed me in the back and was always truthful in his dealings with me. Him, Taity and Jimmy Lowes are top men. In fact most of the people I coached are. Most of the fellows I handled were good men, a pleasure to be with. They can trust you and you can trust them. When we did the *This is your Life* television programme for Jonathan Davies, Martin was supposed to be coming to the studio in my taxi and he was late. I gave Martin a call and said 'Martin, get your arse down here'. He said 'I never thought I'd hear Douggie Laughton telling me to hurry up again'.

Some people accused Martin Offiah of lacking bottle. I ask them: 'Can you get me 10 more of him please?' If he'd been a yank he'd be a billionaire. Same goes for Henry Cooper. We're terrible with our sporting heroes in this country. We try to pull them down instead of putting them on pedestals. These critics have feet of clay.

Martin was definitely my best signing ever (are you happy now mate?) and I used to enjoy watching him play. When he scored the 10 tries against my Leeds side I did say: 'I wish I'd left the bugger in London' but it was said in jest in the players' bar after a bad defeat. I said it to his face as well, he was upset by it. He thought I had taken umbrage with him, but I never did. He said in his book, though, that the next time he saw me everything was fine. He knows what I'm like and that I speak from the heart. I never took it to heart when he told me he was going to leave my club! If I hadn't liked the bloke I wouldn't have fed him at Christmas. I wouldn't have missed Martin for anything. At the end of the day he's a lovely man. He's never done me anything but good and he was a pleasure to have round at my house. We had the same weird sense of humour too; we would be giggling a lot.

I never changed with Martin and he never changed with me. That's the nicest thing you can say about the man. He came to my wife's funeral and we were mates again like old times. People have said that it was like a father and son relationship but instead I think we were, and are, mates. I'm not his dad but would be proud to have him for a son.

Management

Top: Every speccie has a question – even the young ones.

Bottom: Looking cheerful on the bench – we must have been winning.

(Photos: *Widnes Weekly News*)

Jonathan Davies – one of Doug's greatest signings.
(Photo: Widnes Weekly News)

Widnes versus Canberra 1989

Celebrating a great victory.
(Photo: David Williams)

Action from the game.
(Photo: David Williams)

10. Signing Jonathan Davies, the Prince of Wales

In 1988, I knew we were playing great stuff, yet we were getting gates of around 6,000 and we needed 8,000 to survive. In those days I was about the only coach who used to balance the books and to do this I had to sell to buy. Wigan were getting twice the home crowd we were and we couldn't compete, because they were getting a lot more money through the gate than us. I came out with this stupid statement in the press that Marilyn Monroe doing a strip at half time wouldn't increase our gates. I got some stick in the local paper over that. I thought that I would have to counter that and that's when I first thought I'd try to sign Jonathan Davies, the Prince of Wales.

I watched him play his first Union game for Wales on television in a pub near my house and thought he was special. He went on to become captain of Wales. They were playing very poorly at the time and he was getting all the blame. I thought he needs a friend and I can be your best friend or your worst enemy. I rang him. It was 10am on a Sunday morning after Wales had lost to Romania on the Saturday and I told him I would be with him around 2pm. With my club-sponsored car I knew I would have to park behind a pub, leave my wife and kids there and walk the rest of the way to avoid being spotted. Jonathan lived in a little village.

After the Welsh defeat to Romania, the media were giving the captain, Jonathan, most of the blame. But the two rugby codes have one striking similarity. If your pack gets laid on there's nothing much left for the backs.

Jonathan was not very keen to see me. However I told him: 'We are only going to talk, what harm can it do your career?' I told him I would not be taking him north in shackles, it was his career and his decision. Furthermore I reiterated that if the news got out that Widnes and that Laughton fellow were keen to sign him it would take some pressure off him and even if he turned me down his esteem in Wales would rise from turning me down. In sales speak it's called getting a foot in the door.

Jonathan is a smart little cookie and saw the wisdom in this, thus the reason he invited me down. So I had a preliminary meeting with him and he made me a cup of tea. I told him that it cost nothing to talk and asked him if he would like an offer. He said not really and I said that I'd parked my car behind the pub, but could run it through the village of Trimsaran if he wanted me to. He said I had told him that an offer wouldn't do him any harm. I said: 'You're in the same situation whether I make you an offer or not'. I also told him that the Welsh Union side was not up to the job and that if they couldn't win with him, they certainly wouldn't win without him. As it happened, after Jonathan had left, the Welsh Rugby Union team went through their worst spell in history.

I told him that what I would do was to go back home, get an offer from the club and come back and put it before him. He didn't know at this point that I had been on sales courses.

The matter was put to the club and I returned to Wales with Jim Mills and warned Jim that when I rubbed my nose he wasn't to speak because the point I rubbed my nose would be the time where Jonathan would give me a yes or no decision.

I said: 'Right then Jonathan, give me the figure it would take for you to come and sign for Widnes'. I rubbed my nose and Jonathan just sat there smiling, because he didn't really want to do it. He told me that if he got 'x' amount over three years then he would do it. I asked him what time he would be going to bed that night and he told me midnight. I informed him that I would call a special meeting of the club and work like a Trojan to try and get that money for him before then.

I asked him: 'Do we have a deal if I get the money together?' and he said 'Yes'. You don't go back on your handshakes; I was consolidating the deal all the time I was with him. I got in the car and Jim said 'You could have given him that amount there and then'. I replied 'If I did that he'd want more. You've never done this before, I've done it loads of times. You know yourself that if we'd gone for his first figure straight away he would have asked for more. And we've got to see his solicitor and he will want money'. Actually, Jonathan's figure was £5,000 more than had been agreed by the committee, so I really did need to contact them. Jim was of the opinion that this was big business and we shouldn't lose the deal for £5,000. I pointed out that the chairman, Ray Owen, would be annoyed with me if I didn't keep him informed. I rang Ray. He said: 'What does Jim think?' I said: 'Jim says we should sign him. You've got his vote'. Jim smiled. I also knew that Jim had about half the votes as did Ray, the politics involved thought I. Jim asked me: 'When you rubbed your nose, how long was he quiet for when you asked him what he wanted?' I told him it had been about 90 seconds. Jim said: 'It felt like half an hour'. Jim had been dying to speak.

A pub in Llanelli

Jim and I went to the pub after seeing Jonathan. I had decided I would ring Jonathan about ten to twelve just to make him sweat a little bit. But the landlord said: 'Jim, what are you doing here?' We had turned up in the Llanelli RFC chairman's pub. Jim introduced him to me. Norman Gale, the chairman of Llanelli, from whom we were about to capture Jonathan. 'Lovely to meet you,' I said. 'You're not after Jonathan are you?' he asked. Our hearts collectively missed a beat. I took a drag of my fag and said: 'Well, I can't tell you who we're after but it's definitely not Jonathan'. Jim and I headed to a corner. I called Jim a couple of unsavoury names and berated him for not looking above the door to see whose pub we were about to enter.

Anyway, at ten to twelve, I borrowed Jim's mobile and rang Jonathan. 'I think we're on' I told him, 'We'll meet you tomorrow and see your solicitor'. Jim asked me if he could tell his dad yet and I replied strongly in the negative, because it wasn't on the dotted line yet. Until we had it signed we had to keep it quiet. We were staying at Jim's dad's house and Jim told his dad that Jonathan had knocked us back. His dad replied: 'You'll never get him'. So we went off to the solicitors the next morning and we got the deal done. Jonathan asked us what time we were going to announce the deal and I said it was up to him. He said he would like to tell his family and friends before it was announced and I said that was fine. Jim, at this point, was desperate to tell his dad so we went to his dad's house to tell him the news. He said: 'Well done, the boy's a genius'.

When the signing was announced the proverbial hit the fan. We announced the deal on our way back from Wales and the media hype was astounding. We had the radio on and it was being mentioned every five minutes, especially on the Welsh stations. I knew it would be big. It was great: you need to promote your club and game, bang the drum. After all:

'He who whispers down the well,
about the wares he has to sell,
will never reap the silver dollars,
like he who climbs the tree and hollers'.

I helped Jonathan cope with the pressure by just being myself. A lot of Welsh players who went to other clubs have told me they wished they had signed for me. One was David Watkins although I told him that if he had he would still have got where he ended up, only two years quicker. He made it in the end in fine style.

I heard of one Rugby Union international centre who signed for a top club, was given a rule book and told he would be in the first team that weekend. He was also told by the coach that he didn't want him and that it was the board of directors who had signed him.

Davies cost me more than any other player so it was in my own interests to make it work and I had promised him I would look after him. Jonathan's first fee was approximately a third of the whole sum and the rest was over three and a half years. However, what made his signing special was where we normally had 4,000 in the ground for a fixture such as Salford, we were now getting 14,000. His initial signing-on fee was paid for by the extra admission money we were getting.

He made his debut on 15 January 1989, against Salford. It was a mega day. I put him on the bench. The club chairman came down at half time and said I had to put Davies on. I said it wasn't his decision to make, that I had told the media he would be on the bench and unless we got a 12-point lead he wouldn't go on. The chairman was distraught because he felt that the big crowd who had turned up to see Davies would rip up the stands. There were people there from all over the world, it was big news.

I was being mithered by the committee during the game to put him on, but it was a tight match. The main priority was winning the game. I turned round to someone and said: 'The crowd will just have to come again next week to see him'.

Jonathan, the poor bugger, had lost half a stone when he came over to us, he was sat on the bench as nervous as hell. He said he wasn't but I could tell. If it had continued being a tight game he wouldn't have got on and people could have complained all they liked, simple as that.

Anyway, with 20 minutes to go we had a 12-point lead and I sent Jonathan on. I told him not to do any tackling, push defenders to one side, keep out of the way but if he saw a gap, to run. You get no medals for your first game. In the end, we won 50-8, with Martin Offiah scoring four tries.

When Jonathan first came north, I presented him with a number 14 shirt as an example of my sense of humour. We had Tony Myler at stand off and I said to Jonathan when trying to sign him: 'You are wise to come to us because you're not sure of getting a game. It's better than going to somewhere where they can't win a game and send you on to do it for them. We will win whether we sign you or not so it's got to be easier for you. I wouldn't be paying this kind of money if I didn't think you could make my first team. I don't think you'll make number six because we've got an outstanding stand-off but his problem is that he gets injured a lot.' Tony was incredibly tough and I would tell him when he was half held in a tackle to get on the floor and not leave his back open for everyone to have a whack at him. I used to cover up; he never did and was always getting injured.

Jonathan's best position in Rugby League was either full-back or centre. I was never concerned about Jonathan's lack of size, because he knew he would build up by doing weights. Weights were not used in Rugby Union in those days. He lost weight initially when he came to Widnes due to all the stress. I knew he would be successful before I signed him, and after his first game that was reinforced because he had made a cracking break. I knew it wouldn't take him long to get to grips with the game. He's a bright man. He would make a great coach if he wanted to although he might be a bit too smart to fall for that job. He's got his television work now and that's easier. I remember that Alex Murphy had a bit of a go at Davies in the press for not signing for him at Saints. I responded by saying that the next time Saints wanted a signing from Rugby Union I would do it for them. They missed out on Offiah and Davies and gave me £45,000 for one of my other small signings, Brimah Kebbie when Mike McClennan was the coach there. I was dancing around my house with that one. What a coup that was. If I'd stayed at Widnes I don't think Saints would be as good as they are now because I would have kept on doing this to them.

Peter Moore of Canterbury later contacted Jonathan about having a short spell there and Jonathan agreed to go. Jonathan came to see me and said 'Canterbury have sent me these forms but there's no money on it.' I told him to sign it and send it back. He told me he wouldn't sign it if there was no money on it. I told him that was the best thing he could do. I said if I know Peter the 'Bullfrog' he'll announce the signing and once he's done that he's going to be desperate to have you there.

I asked Jonathan if Peter had mentioned money and Jonathan said they had mentioned £12,000 but it wasn't on the form. I told Jonathan he would get three times that if he did it my way. So I contacted Peter and said that Jonathan wouldn't come for £12,000. Peter asked me what I thought he would come for and I gave him a figure. He asked me if I could get the price down a bit. I bartered with Peter over the phone and settled for exactly what I told Jonathan he would get: three times the original offer.

The only thing was that Jonathan never even sent me a postcard or brought me back a stick of rock! I'm not bothered about it though, it's just nice seeing him, he's a mate. He's enjoyed being with you and you've enjoyed being with him.

I should have said to the other Rugby League teams: 'I'm not playing Jonathan unless you pay us £2,000' because everybody's gates went up when he was playing. We averaged 8,500 that year. The population of St Helens is about 280,000 and the population of Widnes is about 80,000 so we got 10 per cent of our town's population watching us and Saints, even today, are getting less percentage wise. Looking at it that way, we were doing well. One in 10 people in the town were coming to watch us. We used to get a few Saints speccies and fans from other areas watching us as well because they felt that Widnes would give them a better game to watch.

Recently, Jonathan appeared on *This is your Life*. It was nice to see there some lads who asked if I remembered them. I didn't want to lie so I said I didn't, but they seemed familiar. It turned out they were from Jonathan's village and had come up to Widnes in a bus for a match when Jonathan signed.

After the game they had wanted to come in the players' bar, but each player only had two tickets to give out. The rules were strict and if I gave Jonathan extra tickets I would have had to have done it for every player but I let them in anyway and took the consequences.

They reminded me that before they left to go home to Wales I had led the singing on the bus in Welsh: 'Blood, blood'! They are the only words I know in Welsh though. If you sing these two words off the others go. They said it was a great night and I was a nice man. I'm not a nice man, I'm a man.

The other thing about *This is your Life* was getting to bed at 6am only to be awakened an hour later by a phone call from big Jim wanting to go down for breakfast. Of course the best thing about being on the programme was when Jonathan walked through the door he said: 'Oh Douggie's here'. He was made up to see the Rugby League lads there. He said afterwards he knew he could rely on all of us just to say what we meant.

The 1975 Challenge Cup Final
Top: With my mother and sons Elliott (in hat) and Douglas
Bottom: Champagne and an interview after the game

91

On the attack for Widnes against Leeds – Wembley 1977.
(Photo: Aaron Agencies Studio)

Top: Wembley 1975 with the Cup.
(Photo: Aaron Agencies Studio)

Bottom: Widnes September 1979, with the Challenge Cup,
John Player Trophy, BBC2 Floodlit Trophy and the Lancashire Cup.
These were all won in the 1978-79 season, when Doug was player-coach.
Shortly after this photo was taken, Doug retired from playing.
(Photo: Aaron Agencies Studio)

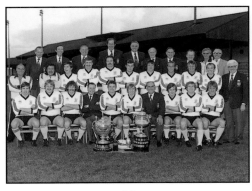

Bradford Northern versus Widnes – 1990 Premiership Final at Old Trafford

Widnes 1989-1990 squad – World Champions

June 1991: Welcoming Bobbie Goulding to Leeds. Sadly, things did not work out for him at the club, and he was only there for one season. He then went to Widnes in exchange for Alan Tait.
(Photo: *Yorkshire Evening Post*)

Leeds: Celebrating with Ellery Hanley and the players
(Photo: *Yorkshire Evening Post*)

Watching training at Leeds
(Photo: *Yorkshire Evening Post*)

In the dugout at Leeds (Photo: *Yorkshire Evening Post*)

Opening of the Widnes Legends Bar: Keith Elwell, Doug Laughton,
Fred Higgins, Jim Mills, Mick Burke and Frank Myler.
(Photo: *Widnes Weekly News*)

11. On top of the world

When I went to sign Welsh international Rugby Union forward Paul Moriarty in March 1989, he was playing at Ynysybwl. I went to watch him and I couldn't get into the player's bar, they stopped me. I was staying a couple of miles up the road and had gone to the bar with the fellow who owned the hotel I was staying in. But because I was from Rugby League they wouldn't let me in. It really annoys me, that type of thing. I asked the fellow I was with did he know two girls who could do a job for me? He said he did, but they would want paying, a tenner each. So we dropped them outside the players' bar and they were given instructions to get near the blokes with the blazers and ties on at the bar and slag Moriarty off. They came back with words of praise for Moriarty ringing in their ears. The girls had been told that Moriarty wasn't rubbish and was in fact the team's best player. I told them that they had just confirmed that I would sign him for us. It just goes to show that there's always more than one way to skin a cat.

When he played for Widnes an incident happened between Paul and the Leeds player Hugh Waddell. The committee said that somebody from the club should represent Moriarty at the disciplinary hearing and I was nominated. When I watched the video of the game I said to Moriarty: 'you stand on your own two feet. I won't be going because you did him'. Despite this blemish, he did a good job for Widnes and Wales in the pack.

Years earlier when Jim Mills and I went down to Neath to see Elgin Rees, we were barred from the Neath club so all the players asked us where we were going and we told them we would be at the pub up the road. The Neath players promptly followed us because they were dead against the way we had been treated by the club. The fellow who had barred us from the club was about six foot six inches but had no discernible arms or legs, came up to me while Jim was in the toilet and said: 'Mr Laughton would you mind leaving this place and taking your ruffian Mills with you?' I said: 'Just as long as you say that to Jim's face'. The actual Neath players had a lot of respect for Rugby League just as I have respect for Rugby Union. It's always the people off the field in any sport who seem to cause problems, because sadly, a greater percentage of them are arseholes. One thing I've learnt about arseholes is that's what they always remain.

I was staying in a caravan in Anglesey and the television I had could only pick up BBC Wales. I saw Emosi Koloto was in the All Black squad but hadn't actually played for the international side. I thought: 'He looks a good player, I've seen a gem here'. The Chairman and I flew out. To cut a

99

long story short, the plane got delayed and we were only in New Zealand for two weeks.

We went down to watch him play and got there 20 minutes after kick off. Just before half time he got a whack, broke his nose and went off. I thought: 'He's broken his nose, I'm only here for two weeks, I won't see him play again'. Our season was about to kick off back home. The chairman said: 'That's a wasted journey'. I told him that it wasn't because I would go and ask the speccies how good he was. He said: 'Will they know?' I told him I would ask them. I walked into the middle of a section of the crowd and as loud as I could shouted: 'Where's that big useless number eight gone? He's rubbish. Is the soft bugger not coming back on?' They attacked me! All I could hear was 'He's the best player we've got, better than that John Gallagher'. They were like a pack of wolves, I thought he must be a good 'un then. It's the same principle as going to the halfway line at Knowsley Road and slating Paul Sculthorpe, the Saints speccies would jump on you.

We did the deal with Koloto. Unbeknown to my chairman I checked Emosi's date of the birth and he was two years older than he said he was. The chairman still doesn't know to this day. He was 27 rather than the claimed 25, which was still not old and I wasn't paying a lot for him anyway. Unfortunately, Emosi got cold feet about the deal, and so I shredded the contract he'd signed. The chairman was shocked, telling me it was a legally binding document. I told him it wasn't if the player didn't want to come. Emosi was looking at me, I said to the chairman: 'What are we going to do? Put chains on him and drag him back? If he doesn't want to come we're not bothered. We've got plenty of players anyway.' I went off to the toilets leaving the chairman to converse with Emosi. I came back and the chairman asked for a quiet word with me, saying: 'He thinks a lot of you Doug'. I wasn't surprised because I had made it clear to him he could do what he wanted. I then said that I thought he would sign again. The chairman doubted this but I told him I have sales technique and Emosi would be joining Widnes.

We took him out for a steak and a few drinks, during which time we talked rugby. Then Emosi informed me that he had changed his mind and wanted to sign. I said: 'It took me an hour to write the first contract out, I'm not doing it again'. The chairman said: 'I will do it' and he promptly obliged with a second one. I told Emosi that if he went back on this one I wouldn't go through it all again and instead we would be on the plane to Australia never to return. He promised he wouldn't. I said if he did he would get me the sack. He came to Widnes and he was a great player. It was a pity he picked up a bad injury because he had magic hands. If I had got him when he was 19, in my opinion he would have been one of the greatest players to ever play the game.

More Union players

I never miss a signing when it comes to Union. I use a simple format and it still works now. In Union they put the best footballer at inside centre and he makes the decisions so you know he'll be a good player. The outside centre usually has less skills and the fly halves, especially in those days generally just used to lay it off and kick, Davies and current England fly-half Jonny Wilkinson are the exceptions. Wingers will always make it. You name me a decent winger we have in British Rugby League at the moment, Union has the whole world to pick from. Eventually, the more players who start to play League, the better the standard. The props will seldom make it in League, no chance; they are normally just scrummagers. The two flankers on the outside of the pack have a chance of converting to League; and the hooker is usually a big strong animal. I said to someone recently that the hookers in Union can catch pigeons now. Because there is money in Union now people who may have made a living being a doctor or whatever will try their hand at Union.

I was on a roll by the time I signed Welsh Union player John Devereux in September 1989. I realised that I could do with another winger. Jonathan Davies told me that Dev was a good 'un, tough and that I would like him. I went to meet him and his dad with Dai Morgan, a member of the Widnes committee who came with me, being a Welshman himself. Dai arranged a meeting between us all in a hotel, but failed to mention that I would be attending. When Dai introduced me John asked me what I was doing there? I told him that I had come for him. 'You've come for me?' he said. And his next question marked him out as being a little naive: 'What for?' he asked. I said: 'To sign you'. 'I'd love to sign for Widnes,' he said. I asked him if he was serious and he assured me that he was. He turned out to be a really nice man and a good player too. He could injure himself warming up though, he ran into a goalpost once and had to have four stitches on the Saturday before a big game the next day.

I signed Esene Faimalo for Widnes in October 1990 after one of the Kiwi tours. Eddie Mac, my scout, asked me if I had seen him to which I replied I had. Eddie told me that Esene had called him and so I said: 'Let's go and get him then'. He didn't cost a lot. They used to call him the 'Flymo' because he was that quick over the grass. He was a good player.

I had been quite impressed by the New Zealand Rugby League skipper Gary Freeman, whom I persuaded, at Manchester Airport, to sign for

Widnes after the same tour, and then had to rip up the forms because Balmain made him a much better offer.

In 1988, in my first big final after my return to Widnes we were to play St Helens at Old Trafford in the Premiership Final. At the team's hotel prior to the game Kurt Sorensen asked for a word. He expressed the view that he shouldn't be skipper as he had never won anything in his life. 'Well Kurt,' I said, 'the way I see it is either I make you a winner or you make me a loser. Changing skippers before a game is not an option, just get your head in gear, picture in your mind bursting through tackles, big hits and lifting the trophy.' After the match which we won, Kurt was walking round like a headless chicken. I asked him what was up with him? He said: 'I've never won anything before, give me a hug, I need a hug'. I told him that as long as he didn't kiss me he could have a hug. I get on well with Kurt. What people don't realise is that he's a very shy man and they misinterpret this and say he's being funny with them. He lacks a bit of confidence but that doesn't make him a bad person, it didn't make him a bad player either.

Many years before, I saw Tony Myler play scrum-half in a Rugby Union game after my scouts had sent me along to have a look at another player they had been monitoring. Myler picked the ball up in one corner, passed it across the field, linked up again, went back the other side, linked up again and scored in the opposite corner of the field. I thought: 'I'm having him'. I didn't know his name though. I was talking to his dad afterwards who told me I already had his brother at the club. I asked him who that was and he said: 'our John'. I didn't know this scrum-half I was watching was one of the famous Rugby League Myler family. I try to get information about players so I went and spoke to Tony's coach. I said to him: 'I can't believe you're playing a fellow six foot two at scrum-half'. He said: 'You know nothing about Rugby Union, that's where you put your best player'. I told him that he had just confirmed that I would sign him. He said: 'Oh no, leave him with me until the end of the season'. I told him he had no chance and snapped Myler up immediately. What a great player.

The Hulmes were two belting lads. When you build a house you need your foundations and Paul and David Hulme were part of the foundations of our side. They were solid as a rock. They would never lose you a game and might win you the odd one. They gave the same performance every week. They were never upset, caused no trouble and were good lads.

Darren Wright was another good steady lad but I am not being disrespectful to him when I say I wished I'd had a Gene Miles to partner Martin Offiah out wide. There used to be a bit of a Widnes saying that

Darren did Martin's tackling for him, but I don't think that's true. Darren Wright wouldn't have been as good without Martin Offiah outside him, whereas Martin would have been good with or without Darren. I don't think any coach ever had his perfect team. Any side can always be improved in some way.

I went to watch Phil McKenzie at Rochdale one night in 1986. My wife and Colin Tyrer were with me and it was freezing cold. I asked if anyone wanted a cup of Oxo just to warm our hands. I went to get them and I heard a roar. I came back and asked Colin what had happened and he told me that they had kicked to McKenzie and he had returned it by going the full length of the field, and scoring straight under the posts. I thought he was kidding. They kicked off and McKenzie did the same again. I said: 'Right we can go now'. Tyrer asked me why and I said: 'We're having him'. The funny thing about McKenzie was that his agent was on the Rochdale board. He was a good player and another we got for bugger all really.

I got Joe Grima for very little from Swinton in January 1988. He could play, get a ball round the back of the defender and slip it out. He was hard and a big man too. When I later went to Leeds to sign as coach for them one of their officials said to me: 'The Widnes side are all massive and tall', I just said: 'Yeah we have a rack.' We signed big players; I noticed when I went to Leeds that they were about a third the size of the Widnes side. A good big 'un will always beat a good little 'un. You walk out onto the pitch as part of the opposition and look at a big player and think: 'He could hurt me'.

Not every signing was a success. This fellow sent me a letter saying that he had played Rugby Union for Randwick in Sydney, another top club in Brisbane which I knew and that he was on the verge of getting selected for Wales, but that he would like to have a trial for Widnes. I got in touch with him and told him if he came down we would have a look at him. He turned up with his belly hanging over his shorts.

I told him to go away, lose the belly and we would look at him again in six weeks. He came back in six weeks and I decided to give him a run in the 'A' team. I was talking to the 'A' team coach, Warren Eyres and inquired: 'How's the Welsh lad shaping in training?' Warren was to say the least a dry bugger. 'Not bad' came the reply, 'He's not lightning, but he's not slow.

Furthermore he says he can kick goals from anywhere, even inside his own half. His kicking out of his hands is like launching a Sputnik and his length-of-the-field kick really does go the length of the field.' So I decided to give him a run in the 'A' team.

The club was buzzing, most of the first team squad came to watch him. He ran out of the tunnel, but some joker had kitted him out with these American Football style massive pads plus a huge skull cap. I remarked to the first team players: 'That's not very nice'. Anyway, we scored 10 yards to the left of the sticks and he put the ball down to take the conversion. His right leg was at a right angle to his body while lying full length on the pitch. He then proceeded to throw a blade of grass in the air to check the wind. He whacked the ball and it wouldn't have cleared a garden shed. I remarked that it was 'probably nerves'. In the next few minutes he received the ball and was running down the wing when he got clattered over the touchline. He was on the floor writhing in agony and squealing like a stuck pig.

The medical staff were carrying him from the field when we scored under the posts. The fellow gesticulated towards the goal posts. 'What's he saying now Doug?' Tony Myler asked. 'I would have kicked that one' suggested I. I visited him in hospital where he had a sprained ankle. I paid him up and sent him packing. No doubt on his CV he has now added: 'Played for Widnes RLFC'.

Even some of the first team were not easy to manage. I took Andy Currier and Barry Dowd to a hypnotist. At the time I felt it was my only option left for the two youngsters. I thought that Andy and Barry never listened during team talks. I felt that Andy would be looking at the stars thinking: 'Why should I worry about this game? I'm looking at the stars, I'm on a higher plane'. And Barry would be there with him chatting away and paying no attention to what was going on around them. Of course, that was just part of the make up of the place. No wonder I went grey. Reggie Bowden, who was helping with the coaching for no remuneration, came to the hypnotist with us. The hypnotist gave me a word which he said would gain me their attention each time I said it. Reggie thought that it was a load of bull and expressed his scepticism in strong terms. On the way home I said the magic word and both players' heads shot round and gave me their full attention. I said the word a few more times, the response was the same. Reggie could not believe it.

Champions

The Widnes side that beat Wigan to the title in 1988-89 scored 726 points, 125 better than the next team, and had the best defensive record in the league. The side was full of pace, we had some good footballers and I think we had a good coach! We had a chairman who cared. I always thought that the strongest unit you can have is your family. If you hit my kid I'm going to hit you. That's how I tried to make it at Widnes. We had a good dressing room atmosphere just like the one I experienced at my first club Saints. You had to have that because then they would all die for one another then.

My coaching manual ran like this:

- Never call your players.
- Never call your board.
- Never call your fans.
- Never say 'the team let me down' say 'the team and I didn't perform'.

You have to remember the day after a bad defeat you have the same players, fans and board. It's about taking responsibility and everyone sticking together. The hardest thing about being a coach is spotting the person who's down and stopping them getting more of a hard time. My rule was: when you're doing great you don't need me; when you're down I'm the first person there.

I remember when I got my bad injury at Saints, only Kel Coslett came to see me. In turn I took Kel's wife to see him when he was in hospital. Do good things and good things come back to you. That experience stuck with me and when I was a coach and one of my players was injured I wanted the rest of the team to visit them. If they didn't go, I wanted to know why, and they wouldn't get picked or they'd get fined and so on. They would all go. But if you need to rollock somebody you should call them into your office and do it and not shame them publicly. You've got to mean what you say too, don't threaten anybody unless you're willing to carry out the threat. Don't put a gun to their head unless you know you can pull the trigger. If one of your players does wrong you tell them that if it happens again they are out of the club. Occasionally you have to cut someone from the squad you make sure you pick the right one, the one who has 'sinned' three times. It sends a message to the rest of the team.

When people ask me about handling the egos of the big stars in the Widnes dressing room I tell them that to be honest I think I had the biggest ego. They were terrified of me and I used to make them think that one slip and they could be out of the building. I didn't rule by terror, but I used to make them think that anybody could go if they wanted. You need to see the problems coming, but stop them before they grow out of proportion.

What made Widnes special was that everybody cared; everyone was part of the club. My mam used to go round selling raffle tickets. And the players could handle my on-field philosophy. It was quite simple: your defence sets the foundation from which you can go forward. I would rather see Offiah run the length of the pitch than 20 big hits. The ball will always beat the man.

I used to get annoyed at other clubs 'tapping up' my players. I never used to do that with Rugby League clubs. I would contact the club concerned, enquire if a player was for sale and if he wasn't that was the end of it. Union was different as in those days the game was 'amateur'.

My chief scout Eddie MacDonald would do all the 'tapping up'. If I got a complaint about it I would inform them that he used to talk to everybody. Eddie MacDonald was known as 'Tonto' by the lads because he was the chief scout. What he did best of all was look after any new players I signed. When I brought someone over from the other side of the world he would look after them like a baby. He'd help sort out their houses, cars and everything. The first time I went to an Anglesey training camp with Widnes, Eddie did the cooking which was fine, except nobody had ever told Eddie that he couldn't really cook. He made eggs that were swimming in fat and I was trying to get the boys to eat healthily.

My best assistant was definitely Colin Tyrer. What you need in an assistant coach is first, he's not after your job: he knows his capabilities. He needs to be a nice man so he can relate to people. He shouldn't agree with everything you say because there's nothing worse than that; and you end up thinking you're right about everything. Tyrer and I used to have blazing rows. I remember an 'A' team cup final at Rochdale. Tyrer had Tony Myler on the bench coming back after injury. Widnes were losing at half time and I went down to the dressing room to be told by Colin that they would be alright. I said that they wouldn't and needed to put Myler on. Colin wouldn't do it so just after half time I went down and said 'Colin you're overruled, Myler is going on'. Tyrer was livid and said we would have words after the game. Anyway, Tony went on and won the game for them. I thought after the game that Colin was going to have a right go at me because he had no fear. He simply said 'Thanks for that mate, I was being a pig'.

Andy Gregory

Colin also used to pester me like mad after we signed Andy Gregory, arguing we should put him in the first team. I told him that Greg would have to work before he got his chance. I was keeping Greg down on purpose. I knew that when Reggie Bowden went to Fulham that Greg would be ready to step straight in. An 'A' team coach gets everyone who's been dropped from the first team and they all whinge so he's got to be a nice man and a listener. I'd just say 'You're not playing in the first team because you're not playing well enough, don't come crying to me', whereas Colin would say to them 'Well you're getting a game in the 'A' team and if you do well Doug will give you another chance'. The worst thing about the 'A' team job is that as soon as you've got a good 'un the first team coach will whip him off you. Colin's 'A' team could be top of the league, I would take his best two players and he was back to struggling again. 'A' team coaches must have good knowledge of the game to cope with all this.

I would always try to help players who had problems. The problems would vary in nature and some I couldn't help. If they admitted to something they'd done wrong that was one thing but if they tried to lie their way out of something I wouldn't help.

I used to encourage competition between players in training. I thought it was a healthy thing to have. People would ask if having a team filled with such flair meant that I ever wanted them to 'shut up shop', but I knew we were in the entertainment business and I used to like watching them play that way. I would have loved to have played in that Widnes side, but I'd have probably ended up as the person who slowed the game down, saying: 'Let's shut it down now lads'. They didn't have that in them at all; they would fling the ball about like nobody else. It was magic at times. I've never seen rugby like it in my life. The former Rugby Union players always wanted to recycle the ball. That helped make it special.

I never told my players to wind up the opposition verbally. I was never into that side of the game. It used to happen to me when I was a player and I never agreed with it. I don't think there's any room for it in the game to be honest. One player used to do it to me. In one match I put a chip over the full-back and the ball was over the line waiting for me to score. This particular player was chasing me. I waited for him and instead of scoring did him with my elbow. I didn't wait for the referee to tell me, I just marched straight down the tunnel.

The two Challenge Cup semi-finals we lost to Saints in 1989 and 1991 were my fault. I don't believe in luck, I think you make your own luck. In 1989 I told Sorensen what to do and he did it wrong, but that's my fault. He took a dummy off Saints' Les Quirk. My team didn't take dummies, but he took it. I had put the team on something we called 'red alert' which means if a player dummies you shouldn't take it. We were devastated but it happens. I've learnt not to look back because you can't change it once it's gone. People ask me what such a good side would have done at Wembley, but it's like asking how long is a piece of string - we never got there. As much as you learn, you sometimes forget the important things.

The biggest game of the year used to be the Challenge Cup Final at

107

Wembley, it didn't matter if you'd won the league, Wembley was the big thing. In Wigan during Wembley week, the whole town changed. That's the biggest thing I noticed at Wigan - when we got to Wembley, the town came alive. You also trained differently. That's what I brought with me when I left Wigan to go to Widnes. I think that's one of the reasons that Widnes went to Wembley so many times in the late 1970s. At this point in my life though, I was running my own business, coaching Widnes, buying and selling players, I had too much on my plate and forgot to focus on the big one. We were the best side in the game at that time I thought, so blame me for not being focussed enough to take the team to Wembley.

The three Premierships Widnes won on the run, 1988, 1989 and 1990, to be honest, were a kick in. We were expected to win. When you're on that sort of roll, it's hard to take you off it. You don't seem to get any injuries when you're buzzing, I don't know what it is, everybody wants to play. What I did learn in my coaching career is that when the side is struggling and times are hard that dead leg becomes a broken leg and if you are winning the same leg is fine.

It was not healthy for the game when Wigan became so dominant. I remember I had Kelvin Skerrett sat in my living room and I knew basically that we had a deal to sign him. But then we lost him to Wigan, who had more resources than us.

World Club Challenge

The standout game of my coaching career and probably the best game I have ever seen would have to be the World Club Challenge where Widnes beat the all star team of Canberra Raiders 30-18 at Old Trafford in October 1989. Before we got to play Canberra though, in May we took on the French side St Esteve for the European Championship, to decide the northern hemisphere representatives for the World Club Championship. We won 60-6 in front of 350 people in Arles. How bad was that? The idea was that if they sent us there we might not be able to play Canberra.

St Esteve were no Canberra who had Mal Meninga, Laurie Daley, Ricky Stuart, John Ferguson, Bradley Clyde, Glen Lazarus, Steve Walters and Gary Belcher. It was like an international side. They did a press call at Old Trafford and I went to see them out on the pitch. One of my coaching staff asked me what they were like and I said don't tell the lads, but they'll get 50 against us. The way Canberra had thrown the ball around was frightening and I knew it was going to take an almighty effort to stop them.

108

When I spoke to the lads, remembering this is a clean book, I said: 'They've all got more skill than I had, you lot are Donald Ducked, you might as well throw the towel in now'. The players sat there with their heads down. I told them that they would just have to keep hanging in there, keep going, keep working in defence and keep playing rugby. I said that Canberra would come out like a storm and if we could weather that storm we would get them. Having said that, I didn't think we'd be 12-0 down after just 12 minutes. We just needed to keep scrambling and working hard. I honestly believe if they'd have got another 20 points we would have done the same. And at the end of the game, if it had gone on for another 10 minutes we would have scored another 20 points as their heads were down.

That's the sign of normal people, there are no supermen. The Aussies aren't supermen, they just give it all this psyche all the time. They psyche the England cricketers every time before they play them and it always comes up a treat for them. It's not very British I suppose, it's an Australian trait. I remember in the press conference before the Canberra game their coach was saying that it was going to be a slightly difficult game for them but then again they were the Australian Grand Final winners and the game in Britain is of a lower standard. He changed his tune after the game when he said his players had been 'tired'. He also stated that we 'scrambled' well. I felt like asking him what he thought of the tries we scored from our own 25. If I'd been him I would have just said that the best team won. After all the best team always wins. I think I actually said in reply to the 'tired' excuse: 'Well we'll come across to Australia and play it again next week', all the while thinking hopefully that we couldn't afford the airfare.

1989: World Club Challenge: Widnes 30 Canberra Raiders 18

In 1987, Wigan had beaten Manly-Warringah to win the unofficial World Club Challenge. There had been no match in 1988, but in 1989, the match was revived, with the support of the Rugby Football League. Widnes facing a Canberra Raiders side full of stars at Old Trafford. Led by Mal Meninga, it included nine players who won international honours for Australia.

The Widnes team reflected the work Doug had done in recruiting talent from Rugby Union. The backs included Alan Tait, Martin Offiah and Jonathan Davies. The team was captained by second-rower Kurt Sorensen.

109

Canberra only arrived in Britain three days before the match, after a week of celebrating winning the Premiership in Sydney. But after eight minutes, they took the lead, Meninga scoring after a thrilling five-man move. Wood converted. Two minutes later, Meninga put Wood clear, and he put O'Sullivan in to score under the posts. Wood converted again, and after 11 minutes, Canberra were 12-0 up. Wood missed a penalty, and Clyde had a try disallowed for a forward pass, so it could have been worse for Widnes.

But on 26 minutes, Grima and David Hulme put Paul Hulme in for a try. Then five minutes before the break, Offiah scored in the corner. Davies converted, so at half time, Widnes trailed 12-10.

Five minutes into the second half, Daley was sin-binned for a high, late tackle on Davies. However, his effort could not stop Davies scoring. With Canberra down to 12 men, Widnes added two more tries: Offiah and Eyres scoring. Davies converted the second try to put Widnes 24-12 ahead. With nine minutes left, Wright scored and Davies converted again to give Widnes a 30-12 lead. A consolation try from Walters two minutes from time, converted by Sullivan did not threaten Widnes's domination of the second half.

Leslie Woodhead's report in The Liverpool Echo *said that: 'Widnes put British Rugby League football on top of the world with a performance of outstanding character and skill in the electric atmosphere of Old Trafford last night.'*

The match attracted 30,786 to Old Trafford, and was televised in Great Britain and Australia. At a time when Australia dominated the game internationally, it was a remarkable victory for Widnes, and a boost for the game in Great Britain.

Widnes: Tait, Currier, Davies, Wright, Offiah, A. Myler, D. Hulme, Grima, McKenzie, Pyke, Sorensen, P. Hulme, Eyres. Subs: Dowd, Moriarty, Kebbie, Smith.
Scorers: Tries: Offiah (2), P. Hulme, Davies, Eyres, Wright. Goals: Davies (3).
Canberra Raiders: Belcher, Wood, Meninga, Daley, Ferguson, O'Sullivan, Stuart, Jackson, Walters, Lazarus, Lance, Coyne, Clyde. Subs: Carey, Martin, Lowry, Bellamy.
Scorers: Tries: Meninga, O'Sullivan, Walters. Goals: Wood (2), O'Sullivan.

Australians

I was never really one for bringing Australians to my club. Clubs spend a lot of money on Australians and I wonder how much homework they do.

110

You need someone to go over there for a few weeks who is a good judge of playing ability to find out the information you need. You could send me over and I would bring you back some good players. You don't just watch how they play, you find out what they're like off the field and how they conduct themselves. You talk to them to find out if they'll fit in with the rest of your lads. Now you'll only get the likes of Brad Fittler playing here when he's past his best. He's one of their best ever players, and we're not going to see top stars like Meninga come here when they're in their prime.

Laurie Daley, the Australian stand-off sat in my house for an hour while he was here for the 1990 tour. He wanted to come to Widnes. I made him a sandwich and a cup of tea and we talked. He had approached me about the move and I was thinking: 'This is going to be one good signing'. Then he said he could only come over for 12 weeks. I said: 'Laurie, you've just wasted an hour. It's been lovely to meet you but 12 weeks isn't going to work'. We never even got on to discussing how much he wanted because it wasn't worth it. If he had come for 12 weeks it would upset the bloke whose place he took during that time. It would take him four weeks to settle in and when he went you would wonder what to do because he'd played so well for you. I'd have signed him for a season though. I'd have got the money somehow. What a player.

I once got into a slanging match with then Australian coach Bobby Fulton. I like Bobby though, he was a great player, good coach, good man. It was when the Australian test side was over playing Great Britain, I thought I'd try and help our lads out by putting a bit of pressure on him. It didn't work - they stuffed us in the test match. He had said our lads had been gouging, so I responded by claiming he picked his team with a dartboard and that deputy scrum-half Ricky Stuart must think that his dart has no end on it because he was never picked. I can be acid when I want but it was just a bit of fun. He started saying that I had problems in my personal life so I just let it go. He probably hates.me now, I don't care.

Moving to Leeds

Leeds came in for me and I wasn't that interested. I had a team at Widnes that I enjoyed coaching and watching. I felt secure with the committee and the chairman Ray Owen who was a fine chairman. In the early days he was ill for six weeks. We played about 10 games and didn't lose one. He came back and rang me saying he wanted a word and would see me at training. I said: 'Don't do it with the lads out on the pitch'. The players were warming up and doing their stretching exercises. Ray came out and said: 'There are three things Doug. First, somebody booked a room at the Hillcrest Hotel and didn't pay for it. Secondly, the players' fish and chips which normally cost £42, cost £67 on such and such a date.' I said: 'It might have been a cup match, I might have let the lads have curries or whatever they wanted. What's the third one?' He said: 'Somebody has ordered some sandwiches and not paid for them'. Kurt Sorensen turned round to me and said: 'Tell him to eff off'. I said: 'Don't you ever speak to my chairman like that'. Ray came on side then. Whether you like the chairman or not he's still going to be the chairman of the club. After that, he was as sound as a pound.

Leeds later came back to me and offered me a lot of money and I decided to go. I needed to take the offer, not to save my business, as that had gone, but to make sure I had a house and so I wouldn't still be working when I was 97. That was my only reason. I had to look after myself. It was also a new place, I had been at Widnes so long, I had become part of the woodwork. I needed to get secure in my life, because it had cost me a lot of money coaching Widnes. I needed to get some money back and Leeds were prepared to pay. For the first time in my life I settled for less Rugby League wise. As I said, at first I wasn't going to go, I met the then chief executive Alf Davies, who, like me, was a bit of a salesman, and the chairman Dennis Greenwood. I have always believed in first impressions and remember thinking I could definitely work with Mr Greenwood and this proved to be the case. Furthermore I had neglected my business. The girl on my company switchboard used to have a dig at me saying if all five phone lines were ringing I would take the rugby call first. No complaints; Rugby League was my passion. If my wife walked naked into the bedroom carrying a rugby ball I would ask: 'Who's is that rugby ball?'

I met the Leeds contingent at Wilmslow. The Widnes 'A' team was taking on the Leeds 'A' team. We were 18-0 up at half time and I told the Leeds contingent that it would be 60-0 at full time. I told them I had seen their team get off the team coach dressed like tramps and for a club as big as Leeds it disappointed me. I said you could get a blazer for nothing and someone should make the players wear it. We negotiated my move and they showed me the contract. It was a lot of money involving a house, a car, and a pension fund. They asked me if we had a deal. I said that I agreed with it but would have to talk it over with my wife. I was asked: 'Who runs your house, you or my wife?' I said to them: 'If the wife's not coming, I'm not, I wouldn't be happy'. I said I would talk my wife into coming to Leeds and that I would give Leeds my decision in two days, I'm not one of these people who take weeks to make a decision. I rang them in due course to say that we were on and away we went to the biggest club in Rugby League. I thought in my arrogant, silly way that

Leeds had more money than any other club and I couldn't fail with my coaching and management skills.

The story that I was leaving to go to Leeds broke. I didn't want it to break, but it did. So on the day of our Premiership Final against Hull in 1991 the fans were talking about Offiah never playing for the club again and me leaving. Martin didn't know I was going, but you'll recall he had told me he was never going to play for Widnes again.

Things happen, but I would say I didn't owe Saints anything after I played there, owed Wigan nothing after I played there, certainly owed Widnes nothing after playing and coaching there, and I also owed Leeds nothing after my spell in charge there. But although I say I owed Widnes nothing, I would also like to say that I had some of the happiest times of my life while I was there. The whole place was quite unique.

Widnes stars

Martin Offiah celebrating another try (Photo: *Widnes Weekly News*)

Great Britain and Widnes: Jonathan Davies, Martin Offiah and Alan Tait

12. Headingley - the Mecca

So here was Douglas going to the biggest and best stadium in Rugby League for a press conference. Compared to the facilities at Widnes, Headingley was the Taj Mahal. The press conference went well and then it was the guided tour and photograph session. The gym was awesome; you could eat your butties off the floor it was so clean. The dressing rooms were spacious and I had an office next door which was used by the umpires on Test match cricket days. I remember once needing a file when the cricket was on and ended up having my lunch with the famous cricket umpire Dickie Bird. This was some place.

I had drawn up a battle plan for my work at Leeds, after meeting with a broad spectrum of directors, players, former players, spectators, journalists etc. I put things into what I called my square:

FOR	AGAINST
1. You're new, Leeds will back you with money. By bringing you here they obviously want to have a go.	1. Leeds have averaged about one and a half seasons per coach since Syd Hynes left in 1981.
2. Give the existing players a chance, don't make too many new signings initially, there must be some good players.	2. There's no scouting system in place, only one scout.
3. Start immediate recruiting of youngsters.	3. Be careful with the media until you can trust them.
4. Everyone must wear proper kit for training and matches.	4. At the moment they dress as they like.
5. Start getting the game into primary schools.	5. No schools north of the river play Rugby League.
6. Get the board on side with the players and fans, that way you'll get more backing.	6. The speccies and players slag off the board.
7. Try to be nice while getting the chief executive out of your square	7. The chief executive likes chatting to the players.
8. Don't make stupid promises and predictions.	8. Too much bullshit flying around.
9. Remember always it's a bad time for the club, country and Douglas when clever but deceitful people are mistaken for wise people.	9. Plenty of clever, cunning people about the place.

When I look back now at that square it was pretty accurate. And I must admit that number 9 in the 'For' column was the one I messed up.

Maurice Lindsay had rang me and said that no-one ever gets them to spend their money, but I might. When people ask me how I got Ellery Hanley from Wigan, the answer is simple. I paid him more money than he was on at Wigan. Mind you I think Hanley wanted to come to Leeds. To be fair I don't think it was just a question of offering him more money. Ellery is an intelligent man, great player and good with the rest of the team. I genuinely think he came to Leeds to play for his hometown club and help make it great.

I think the mistakes you make in life are sometimes down to not sticking to the things you're good at. It's no good being a boss if someone else has got all your tools. I had this gift for teaching people how to play a bit better, Eric Ashton had it too. So for people like us, the hardest thing was as soon as training finished I would have to put a suit on and go straight to the board room. But, I was getting paid a lot of money so I shouldn't moan.

There are people at every club - Leeds, Widnes or St Helens for example - who don't want to learn from your experience at running a team, likewise there are good players who don't realise how important they are to the team.

Looking back through the programme notes I wrote while at Leeds is an interesting experience and outlines the way things went pretty accurately. My first programme notes for Leeds came on 8 September, 1991 against Hull where I laid out how I saw things: 'Having come from a family club like Widnes run by a committee, there are bound to be differences. At Widnes I used to worry about the attendances, the lifeline lottery, playing area, floodlights and even whether the ladies toilets were working, whereas here that is all done superbly. It is also a very sound club financially; in fact, it is run like a business as it should be.

Probably the main difference which affects my side of the job is that Widnes wanted a great team on the park irrespective of anything else. I have the impression here that everything else is sorted out and all we want now is a great team on the park.

Certainly I've had no interference, they have let me get on with the job and the recommendations that I've put to them, provided they make sense, have received their backing. So I'd have to say if I fail at Leeds then there will only be myself to blame.'

Just a few weeks later on 29 September I said in my notes for the Swinton game: 'I was disappointed to go out of the Yorkshire Cup [11-6 at Hull] because it is the only medal which I haven't yet got. It would have done nicely to make up my five or six sets! I am proud of the fact that not many in the game have more medals than me, but that's not to say I haven't had some very disappointing times. After all, to be a winner you only have to play once, win once and then pack in.

Some of the hate mail I've had in the past week or so makes me realise that it takes a special person to be happy and stay at Leeds for a long time, but my view is quite simple – if you come and pay your money you are entitled to criticise. I do sometimes wish though that the critical letters would have a different opening paragraph to: "As a Leeds supporter for 30 years". At Widnes I used to have a girl in the office who opened my mail and we had a simple filing system. If it started, "As a Widnes supporter for 30 years," it went straight to the file marked 'Bin'.'

Then on 10 November in my notes for the Featherstone game, I wrote: 'When we were at Castleford, after the match I met my former touring colleague Malcolm Reilly. He was looking resplendent in a grey suit and he said: "How are you? You're going grey, you've got a Leeds blazer on, I was there 18 months and never wore one." I replied I came here of my own free choice, I wanted this job and if you're not going to wear the colours you can't expect to be part of the team. Not only am I part of the team, the way that people have treated me throughout the area has made me feel at home. Not only have they been good to me, more importantly they've been gems with my wife and children.'

I enjoyed myself at Leeds but it was a strange place. I went there expecting to win things. At Christmas in my first season, we were top of the league and we had got to the Regal Trophy Final, the first final Leeds had been in for eight years apart from the Yorkshire Cup. That fact for a massive club like Leeds, supposedly the biggest club in the game was astounding. I remember one supporter writing to me saying 'We are top of the league for the first time in a number of years. Let's enjoy the moment'. I knew we weren't good enough when I read this. Leeds was a funny place, I could do a book just about my time at Leeds alone.

For years at Widnes my assistant was a wonderful man, Colin Tyrer. He was a true friend, a heck of a guy, and, on occasions, a snappy dresser, and I wondered who I would find to replace him when he told me that he would not be joining me at Headingley.

I was in the process of signing a young player that a scout had recommended and which I considered to be ongoing business. I was quite amazed when he said he had been playing trials at Second Division York. When I asked why, he said it was because there was a wonderful little fellow there called Gary Stephens. I asked him to have a word with Gary to see if he fancied being my assistant at Leeds. He did.

Gary had many qualities which were similar to Colin Tyrer's, the main one being that he was great with youngsters. He was a friend to the first team players and would never betray their confidences - to me or anyone else - and probably what made him more in the 'Tyrer mould' than anything is that he is his own man. He had a terrific sense of humour.

After about the first five or six weeks I said to Gary: 'You'll do for me mate' and patted him on the head. He said: 'What's going on?' I said: 'You are doing a great job'. Sometimes in my life when people have been eloquent about me, I have often thought that a pat on the head is a wonderful gesture.

There was a night when the boys were doing a weight training programme in the gym, Gary Stephens said to me: 'Did you do something like this at Widnes?' 'Oh yes,' said I, 'but you needed a scarf round your mouth and hot stuff on your hands, because you were out doing the weights under the stand in the freezing cold!' In fact, probably one machine in the Leeds gym cost as much as all of the ones I had at Widnes.

When I had an argument with one of the players I said to my wife: 'This is a strange place. Everything I say on the radio is recorded, the same goes for anything I say on telly. It is all videoed and all the press cuttings are kept and put it in a file'. My wife told me that I was being paranoid. I suspended a player. At the next home game, in the players' bar a member of the club came to me and said: 'We've monitored everything you've said in the press, on television and radio and we have to say that you've been foot perfect, well done'. I asked him to pass me the sick bucket. However, that's how big business works and that's the only way to do things when you pay people so much money. They are very hard situations to work under though. In my first season at Leeds, when we were doing well, a member of the Taverners' club remarked I must be a miracle worker, but I had it in the back of my mind that there was something not quite right.

I was doing the whole 'Outward Bound' thing with Widnes players years before everyone else started doing it. In pre season we did 'Outward Bound' with canoeing, rock-climbing, abseiling, horse-riding, water rafting, sailing, golfing and training. I was talking to a coastguard who used to be in the RAF and he had started his own place in Anglesey where they did these activities. I used to recruit new players in the summer and the best thing to do with your new fellows is to get them with their teammates for a week. The squad would be split into three teams for the week and if Team A had breakfast first one day they would go last the next day and so on. You had to leave the kitchen clean and would get points for that. The winners at the end of the week would get this little cup worth about 50 pence, but the way they carried on you'd think they'd won the Challenge Cup. It was a hard week though. The players thoroughly enjoyed it. Everyone's doing it now, but no-one used to do that in those days. It was great to get everyone in the side together and at the end of the week everyone had a vote for the best team. The fellow in the kitchen had a vote, the people who owned the place had a vote, the instructors had a vote, the chambermaids had a vote over who had kept the bedrooms clean. After the vote the best side won. In 10 visits the best side always won, and nobody argued. The players kept the kitchen clean, tidied the bedroom, were the nicest lads and they were always the best players. When I went there with Leeds, the organiser said: 'Before we go any further Doug, this lot are not like Widnes'. It showed me the work I had to do at Leeds to develop the spirit we had at Widnes.

Of course we played Widnes in that 1992 Regal Trophy Final and my old team murdered us 24-0, which hurt a bit. Incidentally, my first league game at Leeds was against Widnes courtesy of the famous 'Rugby League fixtures computer'. We didn't win, but lost only 12-10, which was not the usual hammering Leeds got at Widnes. The lads did all right.

On 8 February 1992, my programme notes for the match against St Helens make interesting reading because I think they prove that I certainly know how to spot a player who is going to make it. 'For most of this season I have had coaches from other clubs ringing me up wanting to play "swapsies". This is a game I have played before, although some of them seem to think that I am a rookie at it. How it goes, quite simply, is that they have some player or players at their club who are not good enough for them and they want to offload them onto you and make the simple excuse "we have no money" and they hope to steal a better player away from Leeds. I have upset one or two of them by saying "don't bother ringing me, I'll ring you if there is a particular player at your club in whom I am interested".

One of the things I noticed after my move over to Yorkshire was that the amateur game over here seemed to be way behind the standards I had been watching over the other side. A fact which is probably borne out by the performance of the Lancashire Academy side against Yorkshire. There was a youngster in the second row for Lancashire called Farrell, who was a rave after the game. It may be of interest to supporters to know that I tried to sign him in my Widnes days... Even at 14 he was a giant, and he is definitely one to be noted for the future.' I think I was proved correct as he is now Great Britain captain.

We would have players' meetings at Leeds and none of the players would speak. If there is one thing I do know, I know how to get people to talk. I've read books, been on courses. Then it came to me, the reason they weren't talking was that someone was telling them not to talk. So soon after I joined the club I signed Mike O'Neill who is the most honest man I've ever met in my life. The first Leeds meeting with Mike there saw him saying to the rest of the team: 'How come you're not talking to Douggie? He's a top man, he won't let you down.' Away we went then and everyone started speaking, if they hadn't Mike would have battered them!

I knew who the player was who had stopped the others from talking and I just thought if he's clever we'll see who's cleverer. I'm a great one for waiting.

When I was at Widnes, Mike was offered £6,000 by Rochdale, I told him that I had been to the board three times and all we could offer him was another £1,000. He said that wasn't good enough. I told him I would draw the road to Rochdale for him which involved me writing down 'losing pay, win one game'. Mike went to Rochdale and when they got to the last game of the season and hadn't won, he said to his team-mates: 'We've got to win this one 'cos that's what Douggie said!' In any great side, you have what are known as journeymen. Mike O'Neill was not an out-and-out star, he was the bloke who pulled the ropes, he'd put the same game in every week and never moaned. He was once awarded player-of-the-year at Widnes and stood up and said: 'I've been lucky, I've been really lucky'. I think he spent about five minutes saying how lucky he was to be at Widnes. That sort of person makes the others feel a bit humble. Some people will walk over anyone to do things, think they are too good for the place and that they run the show. They never do though. You need a few people like Mike O'Neill.

At Leeds, a similar player was Roy Powell. You wouldn't have met a nicer fellow. I thought when I went to Leeds though that all the pack were very similar and thought they lacked aggression, not like the Widnes pack of 1975 - that was big time aggression. Roy was a cracking lad and had been at the club a long time. This tells you though at a club like Leeds who haven't done anything for a few years and have gone through a lot of coaches, is that there has to be a change of playing staff. Whatever else happened, there must have been one coach who could have done the business. So if it wasn't the coaches, look at the players.

By the end of the 1991-92 season a lot of stories were circulating and I used my programme notes for the game against Halifax on 17 April to deal with them: 'The truth of the matter is that just because we have a huge band of supporters and wonderful facilities, it doesn't mean that the

120

rest of the League is going to lie down and let us have the points or the trophies!

I would, however, like to bury a few myths-hopefully once and for all.

The first one is that I can do without the hassle. If there was no hassle, Douglas would cause some! I like it here and nothing is going to stop me attaining my goal - to put Leeds back at the top.

Another thing is you know, at a big club like this, there are times when you feel like the boy with his finger in the dyke, or the decorator papering over the cracks. There is such media hype that I feel it is my job to protect the players. However, there are times I feel-if he does that again I'll send him up t' creek baht paddle! My tongue is full of bruises from constantly biting it and I really am dying to fire a few rockets.

I have of course made a few mistakes myself, but when I played the game, you know, there was a legend in the Widnes area called Tommy McCue who took the time to speak to me and said "You are going to be a good player, but remember this always, if you make a mistake it doesn't matter. If you make the same mistake twice, give up the game"!'

I got called for taking players from Widnes to Leeds, but I only took players when Widnes started selling them off. I met Martin Offiah while coach of Leeds, but when he told me what Wigan were offering him I immediately told him I was out of the running for him. I think he wanted to go where Ellery Hanley was – they were big mates. I would have loved him at Leeds. Ultimately, I don't think he would have changed the team much though. I should have gone for Shaun Edwards early on, I don't think I would have got him though. He knew how good he was and had it all boxed off at Wigan. They should have made him player-coach there before he finished playing. The powers that be seem to want some of our great people like Shaun out of the game, they seem to be frightened of them. They're frightened of great people because the midget men can't manipulate great people.

I signed Andy Gregory for the club in my second season there. I have said for many years now that two of the first names at my last supper would be Alex Murphy and Andy Greg - because if nothing else, I'd have some fun and a laugh.

I was talking to Ellery five minutes after doing the Gregory deal and Ellery said: 'We will have to do as we are told on that field now'. Greg, who has had the best Rugby League career of anybody - count his medals if you don't believe me - said to me one day: 'I have been lying awake at night thinking: what can I do to make the job better?' I said: 'How's about losing a stone.' Greg is not only world famous for his playing achievements, he is pretty good with the one-liners. But that took the wind out of his sails. In fact the way he looked at me, I thought he was taking it personally, so I asked him if he had. 'Yes', he answered. 'Good,' I said, 'get a stone off!'

We began the New Year of 1993 at home to Salford, who we beat 38-14, and I was in an ebullient mood, writing: 'I have always felt that the public of Leeds deserve the best players in the game'. However, later in the season there were difficulties.

I am often asked if the 1993 Challenge Cup semi-final defeat to Widnes by 39-4 was down to dressing room problems, but there were always dressing room problems at Leeds because there were people in there who thought they ran the club. At the end of the day the only people who run the club are the people who pay the wages. It's not the speccies, it's the people who have to sort the bank manager out.

On 5 September 1993 for the game against Warrington I highlighted in my programme notes what changes had occurred off the field during the close season: 'Possibly the biggest change this summer was the introduction of Australian Bob Lannigan [as trainer]. To say the least, he had a tremendous effect on the players, especially so with the younger ones. It was not so much that he introduced new things, it was more the way he did them and his infectious enthusiasm. One of the things he did, which I remember thinking at the time: "How come I didn't think of that", was to let the players select their own time slot for coming to the gym, with the proviso that they were in groups of two, or three at the maximum. This meant that he could work with individual groups and get the best out of the slackers. At the end of the day, although we are a team game and we train as a team, there will be certain individuals who will arrive in pristine condition if left to their own devices and likewise there will be others who, if left to their own devices, will turn up in a poor condition.'

In 1994 we were back in the Challenge Cup semi-final, this time against Saints. We beat them 20-8 at Central Park. Before the game, Ellery Hanley pinned up a newspaper article in the dressing room which quoted Saints captain Shane Cooper as not rating our defence. Hanley used to do a few things like that and if it works, it works. I really don't think a lot of what some coaches think is really useful works though. I reckon giving someone a kick up the arse just leaves you with a sore foot. Instead you should get them all dying for the cause, get them like a family, make them like brothers who will look out for each other. That's what I wanted my team to be. I'd just got into the schools at Leeds and I wanted to make Leeds the biggest club ever, and I was on my way to doing that too.

Leeds was different to Widnes though. You had the main board meeting with the chairman Dennis Greenwood being in charge of the club overall. He was a gentleman. You could seldom get to him though. I was in one meeting in front of a sub board where I wanted a decision making on something. But this sub board would always just refer any decision onto the main board. I said: 'That suits me down to the ground, it means I don't have to come to any more of these meetings if you can't make decisions, I'll go to the main board meeting'. I was doing alright then and thought that should work. Sure enough, hands went up and I won.

After this meeting the sub board chairman, whom I still think a lot of to this day even though we had a bit of a fall-out before I left the club, said to me: 'Where are you going afterwards Doug?' He told me that he wanted a word with me and I said that I would be in the pub across the road from my house. He met me and said: 'If you ever use a cheap sales trick like that again you'll be out the door'. I respected him for that although he wouldn't put it in writing. I quite fancied it on my CV. In hindsight I do think the way Leeds did things was correct, even though if I rollicked a player it meant I had to put it in writing.

The Leeds way was probably the best way of doing things though. It meant the idiots never got to make a decision. I remember referring to it at one meeting by saying: 'This carrot that's being dangled in front of me, it's moving, it keeps getting further away'. After one meeting, the accountant, who was a nice young kid came up to me asking for a word and said: 'You speak quickly, I'm having trouble understanding you'. I advised him that he should think quicker and then we would be fine.

We had great facilities at Headingley as I pointed out in my programme notes for the match against Widnes on 1 November, 1992: 'One thing that has been of interest with the World Cup going on, has been the number of Australian supporters who have come along and had a look at the changing rooms and the gym. In fact the [Australian] World Cup squad trained at Headingley and Alfie Langer came out with the statement "they are some sheds, they are"!'

One thing from Leeds's visit to Wembley in 1995 was choosing two of the youngest kids to play there in Graham Holroyd and Francis Cummins, actually the youngest ever. I told them the night before the game that if they messed up I would pick them again next week. They had my backing. I should have said the same thing to the other players, they were the nervous ones. The young ones just went out and played and were a credit to the club, even though we lost to Wigan. Leeds was a strange place but a good experience. I wish I'd gone there when I was younger and learnt my lesson a bit quicker.

Wembley with Leeds 1994

Top: Leading out Leeds.
(Photo: David Williams)

Bottom: Action from the match 1994.
(Photo: David Williams)

13. Ringing the changes

I remember saying once to Jim Fallon, a winger I had signed from Bath Rugby Union in 1992, that he was going to get me the sack unless he pulled his finger out and started doing some work out on the pitch. I love him to this day but I felt that he was as laid back as a deckchair. No-one ever got past him though. It's a shame that I got him when I did and not when he was a bit younger. He was a big, quick man and if I had signed him at 19, I would have had some player. He had all the skills but I felt he was just so laid back. When it came to the big games though, he would go across to the other side of the field to pull off tackles. He was a little set in his ways when he arrived but still a nice man, I'd coach Jim Fallon again but I'd want a younger version. I've never made anyone a great player, they make themselves great but I believe you can help people on the way.

Signing people became more difficult when agents started coming into the game. One agent picked Fallon up from the airport and took him to where we were meeting to sign him. He got out a form that he wanted Jim to sign. I had a look at it and informed Jim that it meant he would be giving this fellow 12.5 per cent of the money. I advised Jim not to sign it because his deal with Leeds was already done at this point. He was contracted to the club for four years, so what good could this fellow be to him anyway? I ripped up the form and the fellow said I had no right to do that, I told him that I could do what I wanted. I was once approached to be an agent but it's not something I wanted to do.

The hardest thing about doing a deal is that essentially you're in the same situation as the fellow you're trying to sign. You're thinking 'Will he do it?' You ask questions to find out about them such as are they quick because my advice to people was: 'If you're not quick, please don't come to Rugby League or you will get hurt'.

When I was at Widnes I would tell players interested in joining the club that if they weren't quick they wouldn't fit in. We turned a lot of players away. I've seen some good players who weren't quick, but not many. John Walsh was about the only one who was world class. Iestyn Harris is a good player too and he's not that quick. If you've got pace it's so much better for you. Because I was quick I used to let people run past me on the outside and then tackle them from the side. On the other hand, you can get out of the way too.

Francis Cummins was a stand-off when I saw him, but I put him on the wing because I had no other wingers. I've always liked Franny and think given time I would have moved him further infield again and given him more responsibility. He's no good on the wing with a centre who can't play and I think his best position would be stand-off or full-back. It was hard work coaching centres who positively refused to run straight and give their wingers room.

I was always looking to strengthen the squad at Leeds, and Rugby Union was often a good hunting ground. I was trying to sign Va'aiga Tuigamala and I kept speaking to his room mate Craig Innes, I asked him if Tuigamala wanted to speak to me and Innes said that he didn't think he did. I spoke to Taity and he informed me that Innes himself was a good player. I went to watch him play and was impressed. I would say though that he was another one who was a bit too old when I signed him in January 1992. You need to get players in their formative years. By the time a player is 26 he's probably met about 10 bad people in the game and is sick of being conned.

Kevin Iro reminded me of the Oscar Wilde saying 'Some people lay in the gutter and only see the kerb whereas I see the stars'. I thought that Kevin always saw the stars. He could be looking up at a bird wondering whether it was a coloured dove or a pigeon while the game was going on. I would be shouting out to him 'Kevin, KEVIN!' in an attempt to get him back into our orbit. He's a nice man and I thought played well in the big games, because it was only the big games that would excite him. Once the game was won, I didn't mind him looking at the stars, but I felt he would be doing it even if a game was tight.

I didn't sign former All Black Union star John Gallagher for Leeds, he was already there when I joined the club. I tried him everywhere; he had had a bit of a bad time really. In the training camp he led everything and was a good man too. But I didn't think he was going to cut the mustard and knew eventually I was going to have to make a decision. I put him in the 'A' team to see if it would give him a bit of confidence. He might have signed at the wrong time for a bad side, he might never have got over the bad start that he made, I don't know. There again, David Watkins signed for a poor side in Salford and made them good himself. Rugby League lads don't generally pick on little players in the opposing teams, but they will target players who could win a game. At Leeds I got a letter about Gallagher from one of our sponsors. It was more of a novel than a letter asking why the lad was not in the first team. I sent them a letter saying: 'There are some things between a coach and player that stay private like a doctor with his patient' which was a nice way of telling them to get lost. The sponsors weren't picking my team!

I was very brassed off to hear one player singing after a 39-4 Challenge Cup semi-final defeat by Widnes at Wigan in 1993. He was going round the training pitch and I thought he doesn't care. When I get beaten, give me a couple of hours alone and I put my new head on then and I'm all right. Straight after the game though is not the time. If you don't care about getting beat then you're going to get beat. But after bad defeats, I sulked for weeks, years on certain occasions.

Bobbie Goulding was a mate of mine and will always be a mate of mine. He has the same background as me. We came from a council estate, where you had to fight like mad. When he came to Leeds in July 1991, a lot of the players were calling me and Bobbie, being one of my signings, was loyal to me and nailed his colours to the mast.

The next year, he wanted to fight my critics at a pre-season training camp. He was kicking off, he did smash the wing mirror of my car; he did it with his bag as he was walking past. He didn't jump on my car or start kicking it; that was a load of rubbish. He came down the next day and offered to pay for the wing mirror, there was no problem. I got a phone call from Bobbie days later saying he had been sacked from the club. I said that wasn't possible as I had been on holiday and as coach would have had to have given the word for him to be sacked. I went to the board meeting about the issue and it was very strange. Alf Davies said: 'There is no player bigger than the club'. I asked therefore if the club did not care about the individual? None of them had been there when the incident took place but I had. The chairman rang me afterwards and told me it was too late and that they didn't want Bobbie back. This was all for sticking up for me when other players were being two faced.

We lost Bobbie and we desperately needed a scrum half and Ellery rated Patrick Entat, the French international. I had seen him play on television, went to France to watch him and thought he wasn't bad. I had doubts about his pace though. He was a good, hard lad, but he just wasn't what I needed at scrum-half. If your hooker, stand-off and scrum-half can't play, you are really struggling. They are very important positions and have to be filled with good footballers. Those three and your loose-forward are the spine of your team. Plus you need a full-back who can come on the ball and cause havoc. The rest don't make up the numbers by any means but those are your important ones.

Gary Mercer, who I signed from Warrington in August 1992, was a good lad. I always rated 'Ming'. He always gave you 100 per cent. He would give you the same performance no matter who you were playing. There are not many people who do that. He would just keep going for you and he was a nice fellow to have round the club - a brilliant trainer and a good example to any kid.

I tried to sign Paul Newlove for the club but he didn't want to come, not to Leeds at any price. A lot of Yorkshire lads hate Leeds. I found that

127

there was a lot of genuine hatred towards Leeds throughout the rest of the county. They all regarded Leeds as the 'moneybags' because Leeds also had the test cricket ground at Headingley. This also had the knock-on effect that every other Yorkshire side would raise their game against Leeds, which meant we played in a lot of derby-style matches.

The hatred towards Leeds would sometimes manifest itself off the park and onto the terraces as I felt it did at the Boulevard when we played Hull. I talked about the situation, which I believed was a debacle, in my programme notes against Oldham on 6 March 1994: 'How anyone can allow microphones to be lowered into a crowd is beyond me. In fact, I would go as far as to say that they were inciting a riot, as proved to be the case with rival fans getting stuck into one another. I have often felt that the battle should be on the pitch within the rules of the governing body and I am sure the governing body will take steps to ensure that this carry on is not allowed to continue. The last place I would have wanted to be with my children would be standing under the score board at Hull.'

While I was at Leeds, Bradford Northern coach Peter Fox was one of my main rivals. Well, I'll tell you what, I have always admired Peter Fox and he came to me after we beat Bradford 33-10 in the Challenge Cup in February 1994 at Headingley with a 22,615 crowd, shook hands and said "well done, it was richly deserved!' It takes a man to do that, and, a bit like me, he sat in the dug out, not in the stands with a walkie-talkie.

We have chatted about that before and there are probably points for and against both systems. Certainly, up in the stand one does not have to take the flak that one sometimes receives whilst sitting in the dug out. That walk from the pitch down the tunnel at Widnes and The Boulevard as an opposing coach was not a very pleasant experience. You feel a bit like a chimpanzee in a cage and sometimes I feel that the people on the outside of the cage are the ones who should be in it.

Jimmy Lowes

The best signing I made at Leeds was Jimmy Lowes; I got him for next to nothing from Hunslet in September 1992. He was a scrum-half but we turned him into a hooker. He's a nice lad too. To people who accuse Jimmy of being a bad loser, I say show me a good one and I won't sign him. I can't stand good losers. It's different when you're coaching because you've got to keep your dignity and, of course, you should do as a player too. But there's difference between being a bad loser and making a fool of yourself on the field. By all means, be a bad loser but try and remember that the game is the thing that counts. It happened to me at

Widnes when we played Wigan in the third round of the Cup at Central Park in 1988. We lost 10-1 and there were two very controversial decisions. On our committee we had a solicitor who suggested that the club should not take this lying down, but produce the video evidence and have the game replayed. 'On the fire with that', said I.

When I talked to Jimmy Lowes about joining Leeds, I told him: 'If you're not going to play hooker, don't come, you're not quick enough to be scrum-half'. And the way the game was going the hooker had, in any case, become as important as scrum-half. Unless your hooker can pass out a good ball you're really going to struggle, he's got to be like Robocop, always thinking. In the old days the hooker was just expected to get the ball from the scrum, maybe do about eight tackles and that was about it.

I signed Adrian Morley for Leeds from the Eccles amateur club in May 1994, on his 17th birthday. He became a top player. I'd actually tried to sign Nathan McAvoy from the same club, but he had been snapped up by Salford so I looked for another star and got Morley for £6,000. I never put pressure on any of the kids when they came to the club. I just assured them that they would get their chance. I gave Moz his chance and he's never looked back, despite his shoulder failing the fitness test. I persuaded the board to give him a chance.

I was going to sign Jamie Bloem for Leeds, but as soon as I heard him failing a drugs test for steroids the deal was dead. I signed him in November 1996 for Widnes. Some people didn't want him back in the game, but he had paid for what he had done and that was it. I do believe that the laws of the land are laid down by the majority of the people.

I had current Great Britain prop Paul Anderson coming through the ranks at Leeds. I remember saying to him: 'I can tell you your day. You lie in bed till dinner because your mam brings you breakfast up in bed.' 'Have you been talking to my mam?' he asked. 'Then you get up and have your dinner at half past two then saunter up here for evening training, but you're so full of food you can't train properly.' I said to him that he would never make it if he didn't get in shape. He always had potential, tremendous size and was a nice lad too, but I needed the money when I sold him and at the time I thought he was a bit lazy. Bradford have managed to get success out of him. I always worked on the assumption that if you're buying in, you've also got to sell; you've got to keep moving things around. Sometimes you make mistakes, I'm not saying selling Anderson was one, but he's done better than I thought he would and I'm pleased for him.

In October 1994, I signed Adam Hughes from the Milford amateur club. I had seen him score five tries for them and for the amount we had to pay for him as an amateur Rugby League player I thought he was worth taking a risk on. I always thought he had potential and the one thing he certainly had was pace.

But the young player everyone was after was Kevin Sinfield. I sometimes wondered why he joined Leeds. He said it was the people at Leeds he liked and that's why he signed for the club. The only two he saw beforehand were me and my scout Bob Pickles. I actually met him in his house and ended up teaching him short steps and how to shut a player down. He signed for Leeds because I was talking football with him while everyone else was talking about money. I went to his house in Oldham a couple of times and all I did was talk rugby. I told him not to worry about the money because we would sort that out in due course and that he should decide for whom he wanted to sign first. I told him that I wouldn't go in a Dutch auction for him against other teams, because it would do him no good. He told me he wanted to come to Leeds to sign. I went to a board meeting, they agreed with what he wanted and that was that.

One big disappointment was that I missed signing Keiron Cunningham for Leeds by a day and a half. I rang his brother Eddie up and asked him about this brother of his I had been hearing so much about. He said: 'Sorry Doug, I did tell you about him, but he's just signed for Saints'. I always thought if everyone was chasing a player, we couldn't all be wrong about him.

14. Goodbye to the Barmy Army

The Leeds Rugby League official website credited me recently for setting up a great youth policy at Leeds, an area which had previously been neglected.

I must confess that when the apprentice scheme was first launched, we had to just fill it with six names from anywhere. I was quite alarmed, especially when I took one training session and asked a youngster what his favourite position was and he replied 'centre forward'. I just liked seeing kids playing the game, however, and got things going. When I went back to Widnes it couldn't really be done in schools because the education powers that be had decreed that losers should be awarded the same medals as the winners. What was the point in playing? I want kids to be playing Rugby League not just in Widnes and Leeds but in Russia, as it is now, and all over the world because it's a great game. It will always be my passion and has been very good to me. If I was a coach I would send my scout to Russia, there has to be some players there.

What we did at Leeds was get the schools playing rugby. When I first went to Leeds I went to one school. I was expecting some Academy players but no-one showed. I had six rugby balls, a load of children and a female sports teacher who was dressed like a punk rocker. I pointed out that the Academy players hadn't turned up, she offered to help out. To be fair she got well stuck in and we managed to introduce 40 or 50 girls and boys to their first Rugby League session. When I returned to Headingley and inquired why they hadn't turned up, they told me that their lunch had arrived late in the pub. That finished their holiday. They had let me down.

South of the River Aire, the schools played Rugby League, but to the north it was all Rugby Union. I love my game, in my opinion it's better than Union and yet I still love Rugby Union even though I think that a bad game of Union is always worse than a bad game of League.

If I wanted to sign a top professional player today I would start at Saints, Bradford, Wigan and Leeds if I had the money. If I didn't have the money I wouldn't be looking to sign players from the bottom of the division. I would sooner go to the top of the next division and see who they had there. If you discover one good player it is worth the search. One is one less position to fill. I believe if you can get five great players you've got a great side. I also think it's good to bring young players into the team and give them their chance. If you bring in a couple of youngsters to the squad who can do the business it keeps everyone else on their toes. They're infectious, they're full of energy and enthusiasm and look up to all the other players. They keep everyone going. I was the same myself at Saints as a youngster - I used to lead everything in training.

I was in a pub up the road when Leeds were in the Challenge Cup semi-final the other year. One of their supporters' coaches had gone the wrong way. The fans nipped in the pub for a toilet break and as soon as they saw me that was it, they were all over me. They bought me a few drinks, which I thought was nice of them. If I ever go back to Leeds for a game I will go into the supporters' bar and buy them a pint. The Leeds speccies were very good with me. Yorkshire people aren't supposed to like Lancashire people, but I came to their club and I was straight with them and they appreciated it. I was honest enough to admit that I was being well paid there.

Super League

Before the 1995 Challenge Cup Final there was the announcement of the formation of Super League, driven by money from Rupert Murdoch's News International organisation. Consequently Super League and the Australian Rugby League, who did not want to affiliate to Super League, went about trying to sign as many players as they could for their competitions. All the Wigan players were signing for large amounts, but no-one had spoken to my players and I wanted to sort out the kids at the club who weren't on a great deal. However, I think that the only person who came out of it well at Leeds was Ellery Hanley who got a massive cheque and left the club. I got a few quid for some of my players, but the big deals had already been done for the Wigan players. Again, I felt that Wigan did very well. I helped a few Leeds players at the time with their contracts including Alan Tait who needed to stay in Great Britain for family reasons, and wasn't interested in playing in Australia. I also helped Kevin Iro out with his deal, at the end of the day if a player isn't happy at your club he's better not being there. If I've done everything I can to keep someone at the club and they still want to go, I just wish them the best of luck and that's it. At the end of the day I cannot make a silk purse out of a sow's ear.

At Wembley with Leeds

We lost two Wembley finals against Wigan on the bounce in 1994 and 1995, and then played them again in the 1995 Premiership Final at Old Trafford and got smashed 69-12. I expressed my feelings on the second Wembley defeat in my programme notes for the game against Bradford on

5 May 1995: 'Wembley is the worst place in the world to go and lose. That was my 10th Wembley Cup Final. I have been both a winner and a loser. I accept that if you enjoy your victory, you have to suffer your defeat. Every time as a player when I lost I blamed the coach! I thought, when I am a coach I will make sure that everything is done right. I like to think that I did that, but I am afraid that 80 minutes of football is what you are judged on and I might add, rightly so. I know that the club is going in the right direction. There have been many changes whilst I have been here, but getting my head around this latest defeat is proving extremely difficult for Douglas.'

It's only now when I look back that I know that Leeds recruited me because they thought I could work miracles with nothing, while I went to Leeds thinking I would have the money to do better things. The twain were never to meet. All the older players who came to the club were on a few bob and to be honest I shouldn't have signed some of those players as I pointed out in my notes for the Halifax game on New Year's Day, 1995. 'In my three and a half years here I have had to make some unpopular decisions. It is probably fair to point out that not every decision I make is the right one and there have been major changes in the playing staff. In fact, if I look at a team photo from this time last year there are eight players who have left: Irving, Maskill, Stephens, Anderson, Scott, Parrish, Gregory and Rose. Of those eight, four of them were people Douglas brought to the club.' I would also add that I was not allowed to sell Great Britain international Gary Schofield.

Union players

I remember Chief Executive Alf Davies telling me that an England Rugby Union international wanted to sign to play League, I knew the player concerned wouldn't make it, but told Alf if Laurence Dallaglio rang instead I would be on my way to see him. I know Dallaglio would have made it in League; that is beyond a question of a doubt. I also tried to sign Jeremy Guscott. I chatted to him a few times and we arranged to meet halfway. The morning I was going to leave work to see him I got a phone call from a woman saying she was his agent, that he wanted at least 'x' amount and unless we could talk some kind of money now he wasn't going to turn up for the meeting. I said I wasn't prepared to talk money at that stage, that I just wanted a preliminary meeting and that we would discuss money at a later date. She told me he wouldn't be coming then and I said if that's the way it was going to be, that's the way it's going to be. Guscott says in his book that he turned up for the meeting. I tried to contact his home and his work number to no avail. I thought I'm not going all the way down there if he wasn't going to be there, I had other fish to fry. In any case, the last thing you talk about is money. The first things he should have wanted to know is: 'How hard is the game? What have I got to do? What are you expecting of me?' You might say you're happy to sign for such an amount but when you find out how hard the game is you might want more than that. The first thing I want to know when I meet someone is what kind of fellow he is, will he fit in with the lads I've got? Money comes later.

I was in South Africa in 1995 trying to get Jonah Lomu and South African Joost van der Westhuizen for Leeds. I spoke to Lomu's agent, he said: 'I want Jonah to come to you because I know you look after your rugby boys'. He'd have made it, he was massive. He needs more ball than he gets in Rugby Union, wingers don't get as much ball in Union. You give him the ball, it takes a few men to stop him and if he doesn't score himself, you use the golden rule: the ball goes out to the other side and you're in there.

However, it was at this time that the money came into Rugby Union, as the game was going professional. I just sent a message back home saying: 'I'm on my way back'. I knew there was no chance of them leaving Union then. I could have had Westhuizen the year before for about £300,000 over three and a half years. He was begging me to get the deal done, but Leeds wouldn't give me the money. He would have made it in Rugby League. He was six foot, I was surprised at how big he was. We just gelled when we talked. When you go to sign someone you test them by asking them are they quick and are they hard. I asked Joost if he was quick and he asked me what did I call quick, I said: 'Even time' and he said: 'Quicker than that'. You can never say, but he could have been the best, he looked special. When I saw him tackle Lomu, who had been unstoppable in the tournament up to that point, in the 1995 Rugby Union World Cup Final, I thought he would make it in our game. I gave him my number and he rang my wife while he was over here with Transvaal. She told me that Joost had rang and I rang him back to hear him say: 'Get me out of this Rugby Union, I've had enough'. I thought he might even sign for less now, as he was older.

Widnes had no money, but they would often have a go with signing new players. We stretched the club signing Jonathan Davies, but if I had still been there I would have got some money from selling Davies. Instead they put his salary up, then cut his contract and gave him to Warrington for free. I thought at the time there's something wrong there. Widnes was a happy place when I was there because everybody cared, I'll not get it again. It was wonderful to look forward to going into work.

The truth about me leaving Leeds was that having lost at Wembley and then annihilated by Wigan at Old Trafford I was inconsolable. Of course, the season was over and there would be a nice break and they say time's a great healer, but... it had been mentioned to me that I needed some help with the coaching and Dean Bell's name was mentioned. I was of the opinion that with losing Ellery a player-coach would be a better signing than Dean.

Anyway I was sent to South Africa to sign Lomu and Westhuizen and broaden my horizons. When I came back, I was informed the deal with Dean was done. I had a drive through the lovely Yorkshire Dales, with all sorts shooting through my mind. I'd been top of the league, got to the Regal Trophy Final, three Challenge Cup semi-finals, two trips to Wembley and one to Old Trafford in just four seasons. I had spoken to the fans after the last Wembley defeat on the town hall steps, when none of the players would speak, and perhaps then I thought it's time to go.

I hoped the fans would forgive me, they had been special. My youngster thought that calling my fishing boat 'Barmy Army' after the Leeds fans was over the top. Those speccies had been nice to Douglas, and nobody will call Leeds to me.

People have said that if it wasn't for Wigan we would have won a few trophies there, but I say if my Aunt had balls she'd be my Uncle. It means nothing. I did better than anybody before me at the club, but failure is failure. I dealt with Wigan's domination of the game in my programme notes for the match against Barrow on 31 January 1993: 'Fortunately, tall trees never reach the sky, and one day they will come off their perch.

I do, however, have an insight into Wigan rugby having competed with them for junior signings over a number of years. They took it as an affront when I nipped over to Wigan and signed the young Joe Lydon and the young Andy Gregory for Widnes. They had started to do something which not many other clubs could afford to do - they threw money into the arena and for the last three of four years it was pretty difficult to sign any youngster. I even had the feeling at one stage that they had a bleep on my car, because everywhere I went they seemed to be there!

When one was trying to extol the virtues of signings for a small time club like Widnes for about £10,000 less than Wigan, to say the least it was a difficult situation.

In my position at Leeds one of the areas I have attacked is the signing of youngsters and that had difficulties for different reasons. The main objection I had to overcome was that youngsters did not get a chance at

Leeds and that we always go out and buy a team. That scenario can also be said of Wigan.

The reason that they became great in the first place was that most other clubs sold them their best players. They then embarked on their junior programme which was difficult to compete with.'

15. At Wembley with Leeds

Under Doug's management, Leeds returned to Wembley for the Challenge Cup Final in 1994 and 1995. On both occasions they faced a Wigan team in the middle of a remarkable run of Challenge Cup victories that started in 1988, and finished in the fifth round at Salford in 1996.

1994: Wigan 26 Leeds 16

This was Leeds's first Challenge Cup Final since 1978, when they had beaten St Helens. The match came towards the end of Doug's third season with the club, and every Leeds player except Gary Schofield had been signed by him. The side included two teenagers: 17-year-old Francis Cummins, who was the youngest ever player to appear in a Wembley Challenge Cup Final and 18-year-old Graham Holroyd. It was lead by Ellery Hanley, who was facing his former club.

Although Wigan were the cup holders, they seemingly faced more problems than Leeds before the game. Coach John Dorahy's job was rumoured to be under threat, and he in fact left the club immediately after their Wembley triumph. The rumours also said that Ellery Hanley was to return to Central Park as player-coach. Wigan also had the pressure of sustaining their unprecedented run of cup victories.

Les Hoole outlines that "The Lioners started the game well and played with a cool and confident air, sticking rigidly to a game plan prepared by their master tactician Doug Laughton." But it was player that Doug had recruited to Rugby League, Martin Offiah, who destroyed Leeds hopes. After 14 minutes, Offiah got the ball near his own line, sped past two tacklers, gathered pace and beat Cummins, Schofield and finally Alan Tait, who had tried to shepherd him inside, but was beaten for pace. His run covered over 100 yards, and helped earn him the Lance Todd Trophy. Frano Botica kicked the conversion. Andy Farrell added a second try, which Botica also converted, to make the half-time score 12-0.

A runaway victory for Wigan looked possible at half-time. However, Leeds started the second half strongly, and came back into the game with a Holroyd penalty, and on 48 minutes Jim Fallon scored Leeds's first try. A try from Gary Schofield made the score 12-10, but Wigan's greater cup final experience showed to secure their victory. A penalty from Botica, followed by another superb try by Offiah, this time after a 60 yard run, with another Botica conversion made the score 20-10 after an hour. A Sam Panapa try, with the inevitable Botica conversion, made the score 26-10. However, Leeds had the final word when Francis Cummins became the youngest Wembley try scorer. Graham Holroyd converted to make the final score 26-16. Both Leeds substitutes set Cup Final records: Mike O'Neill had the longest playing span at Wembley – his first appearance had been 15 years earlier for Widnes. And Marcus Vassilakopolous became the youngest forward to play in a Wembley final, at the age of 17 years and 7 months.

Leeds: Tait, Fallon, Iro, Innes, Cummins, Holroyd, Schofield, Harmon, Lowes, Howard, Mercer, Eyres, Hanley. Subs: Vassilakopoulos, O'Neill.
Scorers: Tries: Fallon, Schofield, Cummins. Goals: Holroyd (2).
Wigan: Connolly, Tuigamala, Bell, Mather, Offiah, Botica, Edwards, Skerrett, Dermott, Platt, Betts, Farrell, Clarke, Subs: Panapa, Cassidy.
Scorers: Tries: Offiah (2), Farrell, Panapa. Goals: Botica (5)

1995: Wigan 30 Leeds 10

This was the first time that the same two clubs met in a Wembley Challenge Cup Final in successive seasons. And the result was the same, albeit Wigan winning by a bigger margin. The game took place at the height of the 'Super League war' which was tearing the game apart.

Leeds showed two changes from the previous season. Esene Faimalo replaced Neil Harmon in the pack. Harmon moved to the bench. Leeds's other substitute was new recruit George Mann, who replaced Marcus Vassilakopolous. In the Wigan team, Henry Paul came in at full-back, and Jason Robinson on the wing. In the pack, Martin Hall came in at hooker, and Neil Cowie in the front row. Wigan were now coached by Graeme West.

Despite Wigan bringing in two young backs who were to have a huge impact on the game, it was their forwards who made the most impact. Props Skerrett and Cowie were dominant, and hooker Martin Hall's runs also caused Leeds problems.

But Leeds opened the scoring in the second minute, with a Holroyd penalty. Fifteen minutes later, Wigan went ahead with a try from Jason Robinson, which he scored after a 35 yard run. Botica converted. After 25 minutes, Phil Clarke put Henry Paul into score. A further Botica conversion made the score 12-2. A Holroyd penalty before half-time reduced the deficit to eight points at the break.

But any hopes of a Leeds revival were dashed four minutes after the break. Jason Robinson took advantage of some poor defending at a play-the-ball to score another long-range try. The conversion made the score 18-4. Further tries from Martin Hall and Va'aiga Tuigamala, both

138

*converted by Botica, made the score 30-4 before James Lowes scored
Leeds only try two minutes from time. Holroyd's conversion made the
final score 30-10. It was Leeds's biggest Challenge Cup Final defeat. But
given that Leeds had finished runners-up in the Stones Bitter
Championship, and had beaten Wigan once during the season, maybe
what this match really showed was how far Wigan were ahead of
everyone else at this point in the game's history. Leeds-born Jason
Robinson won the Lance Todd Trophy.*

Leeds: Tait, Fallon, Iro, Innes, Cummins, Holroyd, Schofield, Howard, Lowes,
Faimalo, Mercer, Eyres, Hanley.
Subs: Harmon, Mann.
Scorers: Try: Lowes. Goals: Holroyd (3).
Wigan: Paul, Robinson, Tuigamala, Connolly, Offiah, Botica, Edwards, Skerrett,
Hall, Cowie, Betts, Cassidy, Clarke. Subs: Atcheson, Farrell.
Scorers: Tries: Robinson (2), Paul, Tuigamala, Hall. Goals: Botica (5).

Doug remembers: 'Wigan had been playing in the Cup Final every year
since 1988, and had built up a great deal of experience. For our players, it
was something new, and appearing at Wembley is always a drain on the
nerves. They were featured on television and in the newspapers. I banned
the players from reading the newspapers before a Wembley Final to stop
them getting nervous.

In 1994, we stayed at the Selsdon Park Hotel near Croydon. But the
players decided it was too far to drive to Wembley from there, so first
thing in the morning on the day, we moved to a hotel near Heathrow, and
had a couple of hours rest there. Lots of sports teams stay at the Selsdon
Park, but the manager said we were the best behaved team he had had
there, which was nice.

The first game against Wigan was close. It was Leeds's first Final
since 1978, and I was pleased to be able to take the club back to
Wembley. I was proud of our two teenagers, Graham Holroyd and Francis
Cummins, who did well for us at Wembley.

In the second game, Super League overshadowed everything. It was a
distraction for our players, many of whom were worried about their
futures in the game. Wigan were too strong for us that day.'

Wembley with Leeds 1995

Ellery Hanley being tackled by Martin Offiah and Andy Farrell
(Photo: David Williams)

16. Widnes: Third time unlucky

Leeds was the hardest job I ever had, I needed some time out once I had left which meant I didn't coach in Super League which started in 1996. What I've learnt is if someone gives you three times the money you're on, the job is going to be three times as hard, probably five times as hard, certainly five times the hassle.

When I went back to Widnes in 1995, we very nearly knocked Wigan out of the Regal Trophy in the quarter-final, but Va'aiga Tuigamala went the length of the field to score for Wigan near the end of the game, which gave them a draw. We gave them a real fright that day, losing 28-23 after extra time. Then we nearly got to the Challenge Cup Final in 1996 despite not being in the top flight which would have been nice, but once again Saints stopped us in the semi-final, beating us 24-14. We had won at Workington, Dewsbury and Hull to reach the semi-final. We were robbed in the semi though by a terrible forward pass decision.

Widnes had brought me back to change things and I think I could have done, but they kept selling players. You couldn't see any light at the end of the tunnel because you knew your best players were either gone or going with no-one coming the other way. It was an exodus. Also, I think Widnes got carved when Super League was formed. They deserved to be in the top flight.

I wish I hadn't gone back to be honest. I'd finished at Leeds where they had tried to change me by saying: 'You have to do things like this'. When Widnes started to do the same thing I should have walked out the second week I was there, but I thought I should give it a go and stayed until May 1997. There was no money, so I used to cook for the lads on a Saturday to try and get a bit of team spirit. It was terrible. The older I got the more they wanted to move me upstairs which I couldn't understand. Widnes wanted me to be more of an office boy and that's what I ended up like. My destiny is in my own hands though so if I went upstairs it's my own fault for doing so.

The last signing I ever made in the game was Sean Long for Widnes from Wigan. I got him and £60,000 while Lee Hansen went the other way. The deal took a lot of hard work. Jack Robinson was the man at Wigan I was negotiating with. I asked Jack for £120,000 for Lee and he said he couldn't give me that. I stuck at this price all the way through, I only agreed to lower it if I got a player as well. Lee was a good lad, but he wasn't international class. I remember saying to Jack: 'He won't do it at Wigan', which made Jack want him all the more, thinking I was trying to keep hold of him when really I was telling the truth. Lee had to be in the

141

right surroundings, Widnes suited him and I knew Wigan wouldn't. He'd only played for Leigh and Widnes which are two little, friendly, family clubs. He'd come from one of the small Tongan islands and I believed that he wouldn't be able to cope with the Wigan setup.

Jack ended up offering me Longy and £60,000 if we agreed to do business with him. He said: 'He's on good money at Wigan so he might not come to you'. But Longy's dad was at Widnes coaching because I had been moved upstairs. I asked Jack for an hour to think about it. It was the longest hour of my life, I just thought 'Woo-hoo!' I remember Sean's first game for Widnes and the chairman, who's still the chairman to this day said: 'He's a class act'. What a talent, he was outstanding. Why Widnes later sold Long to Saints I'll never know. I think if you get one player with Sean Long's ability, then a few others and you end up with five class players in your side, you're cooking with gas. However, by the time Sean left Widnes, his dad had already gone. I don't know the politics. I just know that my last deal was my best one. Sean has had injuries, but to come back like he's done; fair play to the lad.

I suppose with hindsight, going back to Widnes for the third time was tempting fate and the success, good luck and good times I had in my two previous stays tempted me to push my luck. When I left for the third time, the club issued a statement that we had parted by mutual consent. The truth was that I was sacked. I can live with that, my outlook on life is remember the good times, put up with the bad, don't moan. Someone is having it a lot worse than I, so I think positive. I remember that the top goal-kicker Mick Burke, try-scorer Martin Offiah and the player who scored the most points scored in a season, Jonathan Davies, were all signed by me and we had loads of fun.

I was inducted into the Widnes Hall of Fame but it nearly didn't happen. I got a phone call saying I wasn't going to be in it. I know that I can ride roughshod over people if I want something doing and at times I can be arrogant. If I know I'm right, nothing will shift me. If I'm wrong, I'll hold my hands up. And some of that upsets people, particularly committee members; they have long memories when they want to get you back. But at the end of the day I was pleased to be in their Hall of Fame.

I think the best thing about being a coach is when you sign someone special like Martin Offiah. I get a lot of pleasure out of that. If you help a young kid on the way and later in his career he gets to play for Great Britain; that is a good feeling. It makes it worthwhile.

On the flip side, the worst thing about being a coach is dealing with some of the committee meetings. They'd go on for about two hours at some clubs when they really only needed to be 10 minutes. There were no decisions being made, because there were so many there and they all wanted a say. I'd be running my own business, go to training, have a shower and then shoot up to the committee room and only get home at about half past ten at night. I'd much rather have had a beer with the lads.

The lighter side

On the lighter side, the funniest story from my time in the game as a player is when Alan Dearden got a cauliflower ear and I heard him talking to Mick George. Alan was a good looking lad and he said to Mick: 'I've seen the club doctor about my ear and he said there's nothing they can do'. So Mick said: 'Go and see me mam'. He said: 'What can your mam do?' Mick replied: 'Knit you a balaclava'.

Likewise, my favourite quotes from my former coaches are:
Eric Ashton: 'Don't worry, they will tire themselves out eventually.' (We were getting stuffed by 20 odd points at the time.)

Vinty Karalius: 'Hey don't stand behind me. I've seen too many cowboy films, them apaches sneaking up sticking a tomahawk between your shoulder blades.' (I had just returned from a seminar on how to hold a meeting and been told 'don't have people behind you, they will be taking the mickey doing the victory sign.')

Vinty again: 'You lot talk about boozing and ragging all day. I talk about rugby and you're like flies when the fly spray comes out, off.'

Frank Myler: 'Never mind lads; a win's a win.' (When we have just scraped home against a side we would normally thrash.)

My own: Upon my arrival at the splendour that is Headingley, at the press conference I was asked what I thought of my new surroundings. I answered 'I might be too good for this place'.

Future of the game

I worry about the game like everybody does, I worry about Rugby Union too because I like that game. Things have to come to a point where we all realise that we can't afford to keep paying players the wages that we are doing, the money just isn't there to sustain it. That's the worry about today's game but, that aside, I maintain that the great players of yesterday would be great today and the great players of today would have been great in any era. When people talk about the gulf in standards between Rugby League over here and in Australia, they don't mention the fact that other sports have the same problem with the Australians. It's the same in cricket, Rugby Union, and swimming. They are a sporting nation, but when you think that the population of Australia is a quarter of ours, we're doing something wrong aren't we?

The Australians play great stuff, I've always thought that the best form of defence is attack and the Australians play some wonderful attacking football. Great tackling obviously has its place in the game, but it'll never increase your attendances. One of the great things about Rugby League at the moment is the progress of the amateur game. Rugby League will never die because there will always be people around wanting to play it and watch it.

I think Super League is better than the seasons immediately before it when Wigan were winning everything. It was a bit boring then with one side dominating. Where Rugby League scores over Union is that in a season probably about half of the matches are good games whereas in Rugby Union only about 10 per cent are good games and the rest are boring. When one in two games are enjoyable, it's not bad is it? The teams in the top flight are getting closer together which makes the quality of the games that bit higher. We should never worry about changing the rules either. If it makes the game better then do it.

But I still have worries. If Rugby League clubs have all got so much money, how come none of us own our own stadiums? It worries me that so many of our clubs don't own their own grounds and in theory a soccer club with whom they may be sharing could say 'get off our pitch and go find somewhere else to play'. However, Rugby League will always survive, even if it goes back to how it was played when I was a kid where you got £25 for a win and £5 for a loss, it'll always go on. On the other hand, one day it might get bigger than ever, you never know. It's getting bigger now than it ever was. I always said that the amateur game is the right way to spread the sport rather than going to somewhere like Gateshead or Paris, all that money down the drain. We could have had another country playing the amateur game. Think of the game as a chain of supermarkets. If I opened my first store in Widnes my second wouldn't be in Gateshead, you have to spread the game geographically in ever increasing circles, but you get what you've got right first and then gradually move outwards.

Regarding the game below Super League, just look at the impact television has had. Imagine you're a kid watching Wrexham Football Club and Joe Bloggs scores three goals, he's your hero. Then you watch television and you see someone like Eric Cantona and you think 'Blimey Bloggs, you're not a patch on this fellow'. So you go and see the big stars instead and that's what is happening to an extent in Rugby League. There is so much sport on television these days. However, I don't think it's a bad

144

thing at all, I think television can increase your gates if you use it correctly. I think Sky TV is doing a great job in spreading the gospel. Look at Russia and the fact they got a crowd of more than 30,000 fans for an international Rugby League game in 2002. Where have they got the game from? Satellite television is how the game is being spread.

I also think that Leigh could still attract a good crowd if they reached Super League, but how many teams can the top level sustain? I've been the odd game at Leigh and it's been quite entertaining stuff. It's not as good as Super League because the standard is not as high.

We need to get Cumbria firing again in Rugby League. We have had some great players from there. We also need to keep the World Cup going. We should organise it like the cricket World Cup where teams are put in groups. Don't put Russia in with Australia, put them in with Lebanon and Scotland for example. We shouldn't be saying to countries: 'You're not coming to England for the World Cup' when that's what they are dreaming of. I didn't get much money when I played, but I knew I could get a trip to Australia out of it. What I've learnt in my life is that if you work just for the money, all you get is money but you won't get any happiness. If you do something because you have a passion for it you'll have more happiness and probably end up with more money.

Some former players and coaches criticise Rugby League. I think this comes from losing the camaraderie you had throughout your career. You've been a part of this massive gang, all with the same interests, all hard men and all having a laugh. Then suddenly, it's gone. The natural thing is to become a bit bitter and start thinking that 'nobody loves me anymore'. That's the only reason I can think of that causes them to complain, because they couldn't have played the game so well if, deep down, they didn't love it. I think if it's been good to you and you've enjoyed it you shouldn't criticise it. If I see a bad game I'll say it was bad which I'm entitled to do unless I get in for free and then I'll say nothing! If you've paid your money you can say what you want.

Dream teams

I could pick a thousand dream teams. But the only people that I know would get in my dream team all the time who I played with or coached would be Vollenhoven, Offiah and Boston. There's three wingers for a start! Murphy at scrum half. Another was Dick Huddart who was six feet three inches, could eat and drink anything yet still had a physique like Adonis. A flying machine with a great hand off.

145

There were so many other great players, but those ones stood out for me.

The players I like watching today are Paul Sculthorpe, he's the best I've seen for a while. I love watching Cunningham too, and was always a big fan of Paul Newlove. I think a change of club would make Andy Farrell a better player. I think he's been at Wigan too long now and is part of the woodwork. He's a great player, but when you've been at a place too long they take you for granted. And finally, I always thought Gary Connolly was a class act.

People have asked me if I was playing today which side would I play for. I can't answer that because when I was there, Widnes was a special place, the players basically ran the club. The committee was elected by the members, so if they were rubbish they would get kicked off. Now things have changed, I can never see that happening again.

The committee had to be on their toes or they would be out. Now you can get someone who's clueless at a club, but has plenty of money and you'll never shift them. My time at Widnes was the best time of my life and everybody else says the same thing. Colin Tyrer said they were the happiest years of his life and he wasn't even playing there, he was only the assistant coach, the whipping boy. After each game we would all meet up, either with our wives in the Hillcrest or on our own. You didn't have directors threatening you.

My main interests outside the game are reading history books and cookery books. From history I think 'That shouldn't have happened' or 'I would never do that' because you learn from the past. What fascinates me about cooking is that one day it must have been raining and some bloke carrying flour got it wet and saw it turn into bread. The next thing you know he put meat and potatoes in it and made a pie. How good must it have been to make something first?

I also used to love reading Oscar Wilde, I had the *Oxford Book of Quotations*, because I wanted to be more educated than I was because my schooling had been poor. This was mainly because of me I have to admit, not because of the teachers, I just didn't want to do it. You think when you get a position of responsibility: 'Well I need to know about things if I'm going to be coaching people'.

I always enjoyed writing about and commenting on the game. When I was at Widnes I wrote a column in the *Widnes Weekly News* every Friday, programme notes for every home game and a column in the *Mail on Sunday*, the latter with Jack Winstanley. When I was in Australia in 1970, I sent reports to the *Wigan Evening Post* – by airmail. At Leeds, I wrote for the *Yorkshire Evening Post* every week, and programme notes for each home game. On one occasion, Maggie, the secretary at Leeds, rang me and said: 'Doug, you've forgotten something – your column for the *Evening Post*'. She told me they needed it in 40 minutes. I'd had a pig of a week, but asked her to take it down shorthand. I bought her some flowers for helping me – it's nice to be nice when someone helps you. Considering my spelling is atrocious, and that my English teacher at school used to put 'see me' on all of my compositions, maybe I can be excused if some of the pieces weren't of literary note. But they were important in having a good rapport with the speccies.

When people say they don't know what to buy me, I just tell them to buy me a cookery book. The most recent one I got was a Jamie Oliver one, although I thought it wasn't as good as his first. Due to getting his first one, I can make a pizza now, a great pizza. But I can't make everything in it, even though I try all the recipes. When Indian food really started to take off in Britain I asked for an Indian cookery book and my wife bought me the first Indian cookery book published in Great Britain. It was like winning the cup at Wembley again. There weren't many Indian restaurants when it first became popular and it was great to be able to do it myself. When I used to get a recipe I would hunt all the ingredients down, get them all and do it to the letter. I cheat now, but in those days I would do it exactly as it was written. It's different now, but sometimes you would have to travel to Chinatown in Manchester or Bolton to get the right ingredients. The dishes seldom work out like the recipe though! However, my pastry is pretty damn good now: it takes you years to get that right, it's a science never mind an art. You need cold hands to do it. At first it was something to do to take my mind off a big game. Some people just went on the juice to take their mind off the game, I just went and did a bit of cooking.

Another of my long time goals was to retire at 55. But I made it earlier than that; and it's not all that it's supposed to be. Sure, my lawns are good and so are the hedges. All the jobs around the house are done. I can go on holiday whenever I like, and have loads of wonderful memories. I have climbed the big ladders and hit the big snakes. I have finally written this book, and I enjoy sea-fishing in my boat.

I need to develop some new interests. I don't want the stress of management again, but I would like to use my talents to help develop young players. Getting basic skills is so important. I remember how Jonathan Davies used to practice side-steps, and every young player should work at their skills. Retiring is sometimes hard work. Maybe God is telling me he gave me special talents and I should use them.

Wembley 1975: Widnes versus Warrington.
A 'friendly' discussion about the game between
Doug and Warrington's Dave Chisnall. It was a tough game.
(Photo: Aaron Agencies Studio)

17. Memories of Doug Laughton

Hundreds of players and coaches have worked with Doug Laughton over the years. This chapter includes tributes from players and coaches from different stages in his career.

Alex Murphy OBE

Doug was probably one of the best footballing loose-forwards there has been. He was a very high quality, intelligent Rugby League player with a lot of ability, great pace and a good pair of hands. As a matter of fact, he would have been an ideal modern-day player: very quick, good brain and a very intelligent player. What he didn't do when he first came to St Helens was believe in his own ability. The kid had the ability and maybe all he needed was just a kick-start to bring it out of him. I gave him that kick-start on the pitch and also for the team's benefit because when he played well it was like having an extra player on the field. Some times in life you need people to give you that kick-start and he was a young guy with bags of ability and once he got on the big stage, there was no stopping him. We were both at a great club, St Helens, which helped us both develop our style of rugby. You have to be a certain type of player to play at St Helens, they don't just have any Tom, Dick or Harry playing there, you have to be able to play high quality rugby against anybody and Douggie and I could do that. It led you into other things; Douggie eventually went into coaching and became a great coach. Personally, I think he's been the best coach in Rugby League for a long, long time. He has a great talent for spotting players and a great talent for letting players play, which he'd also learnt from St Helens. This kick-start he had at St Helens was all part of that process. Let me put it this way, he'd certainly go in my top 10 of any world-class players without any doubt and he'd certainly go in my top 10 of any world class coaches and very high on that list too.

Kel Coslett

"Doug was a player you'd have in your side every time. He was always capable of doing something good. As a player, he was someone I'd rather play with than against. When I came up to St Helens from Wales, he was a young lad as was I. I've known him a long time and he's always been a good lad. Obviously he's changed as the age goes on but he's still the genuine person that he's always been. When he was young, he was so keen to do well that every time he was tackled he would inform the tackler "If you tackle me again, I will kill you!" He was that type of fellow, he was on the go all the time, fair play to him.'

Eric Ashton MBE

'Doug was an excellent player. I always admired Douggie when he was playing at St Helens, he was a dynamic sort of player, a young, keen player. He picked up a bad knee injury when his knee caught the post in a game at St Helens and in those days this was a bad injury. There are not many players that would have got over it but he did because of the type of player he is. He got sour with St Helens for whatever reason and I was player-coach at Wigan at the time. My chairman was a chap called Ken Broom, a big bookmaker in Wigan and a chancer as bookmakers are. He came to me and said "This Doug Laughton, I've had a word with him and there's a chance he could come here". I said: "Get him here, he's got a bad knee at the moment but we could always insure him against that if things went wrong. I like him, he's a good player". I couldn't praise Douggie Laughton enough.

He was a funny bugger Douggie , though, he wasn't easy, but he was a winner. There was nothing in second place for him. He had to win and showed it in his effort, his keenness and everything he did. There would be times where I would be doing things as coach and Douggie would be thinking "Oh, bloody hell" and wouldn't be at the back of the queue to say what he thought. We did get on reasonably well though as a coach and a player can do.

I think we had the same sort of views on how the game should be played. When Douggie came to Wigan, he came as number one. The great side that I had played in was falling away, the forwards had gone. Barton, Sayer, McTigue and the rest had all left the club at different times. We were just starting in 1967 on a build-up programme. Of course, with Douggie coming along, it built up very quickly because he wanted the best alongside him. He would be saying to me "Go for him, Ash" all the time as he requested new signings. He bubbled with enthusiasm and that's the thing that sticks out with him more than anything. Any person who bubbles like that as a player and as a coach couldn't fail and he didn't fail. He had a lot of success as a coach. He was the same there, picking up Jonathan Davies from Wales and Offiah in London. He's that type of lad.

There's a million tales I could probably tell you about Douggie but I'm not sure whether I'd be allowed to. He was a harum scarum let me tell you that. He was a bugger. If you had 10 ropes, nine would have to be round Douggie's neck!

I am a great admirer of Douggie Laughton and couldn't say enough good things about him. We left Wigan together, I moved onto Leeds and later St Helens. He moved to Widnes. I can remember him coming to me and saying: "Are you staying or not?" I said: "No I don't think so". "I'm off to Widnes then," he said. That was Douggie you see, he would just do it. I said "Wigan will have a say in that". "I'm off Widnes, that's it" he replied. And he was. He was that type of person.

He was good for team spirit, a winner, you couldn't ask for anything better than Douggie Laughton. I couldn't praise him highly enough to be honest.'

Frank Myler

'Doug was a great player. I would certainly rate him in the top five loose-forwards I played with, that says a lot considering I played with Mal Reilly, Vinty Karalius, Derek Turner, Johnny Whiteley and so on, he was certainly in that class. He had a lot of strengths as a player, for a big fellow he had pace, and was a great passer of the ball. He was a good all round player.

He was easy to coach and went into coaching very successfully. He certainly had a brilliant footballing brain and the most important thing was his ability to relate to others and understand others. Until someone takes a job you never know if they are going to be good at it. You can be the best player to ever play the game but if you can't speak to people you're not going to be able to coach. Doug was good on man management, a real player's man. He had done it all himself as a player. A coach needs that personal touch with the players and he had it in abundance.

There are a number of funny stories about Doug. On the 1970 tour the famous Kangaroo Reg Gasnier, who had retired, was filming an advertisement for Australian television for Big Ben pies. There were about 12 of us involved in a mock training session for the benefit of the cameras. We stopped training and started eating the pies. Everything was going well until Reg asked how good the pies were. Doug said they were ok and did he have any more left? The television people were chuffed with this and Reg said 'Yeah we've got plenty' to which Doug answered 'Well that's your fault for making too many'. Of course, this instantly stopped the filming and we had to start all over again. He had a great sense of humour and what's more, an answer to everything.

Top player, top coach.'

Chris Anderson

'I first met Doug at Canterbury, Peter Moore brought him over to Australia. It was only a short stay for him at the club but when he went back he recommended me to come to the UK and play for Widnes.

Doug was a very talented player, with great skills, who could run the ball. He was probably a similar style of player to Malcolm Reilly. Douggie was a tough competitor, I thought he was a bit reserved in the dressing room at times, but I was only young back then. That was my perception at the time. Of course, we both went onto become coaches and when I'm asked whether I thought he was going to become a coach, during our playing days, you have to remember I was 21 at the time and you don't think of that sort of stuff. However, it didn't surprise me that he became a coach because he was always a confident sort of character and always had great skills.'

Reg Bowden

'Doug was a Great Britain international, but he'd had a knee reconstruction, and at one time it looked like he would never play again. He joined Widnes in 1973, and came pedalling into Naughton Park on a bike, with his knee strapped up. We thought we'd signed a cripple. But our physio Mr O'Malley worked on his knee and got it right. Signing Doug Laughton was a great coup for Widnes. He was a tremendous player. I believe he was one of the best loose-forwards ever in the game.

As a coach, you couldn't get anyone better. He used to say "you can't make a silk purse out of a sow's ear", meaning you can't turn bad players into good ones. But what he could do was buy good players and enhance their play – make them a little bit better. He was also good at buying and selling players. He would improve his squad by getting rid of the bad players, and finding better ones. He kept improving the team at Widnes that way.

He had lots of ideas. He always wanted a quick play-the-ball and a quick back up. He wanted gang tackling to knock the opposition out of their stride. He was also a big advocate of fitness. He said that if we were fitter and stronger, even if we were playing a side who had better skills than us, our superior fitness would see us through. Coaches in Super League now have the same approach.

As a coach, I learnt a lot from Doug. When I left Widnes in 1980 to become coach at Fulham, he told me that if I needed any advice, to come and ask him. We had signed some experienced players, such as Ian van

Bellen, Harry Beverley and Mal Aspey, and had the makings of a good side. I asked him what he thought of Eddie Cunningham. He told me I had enough old players, and said the same about Eric Prescott. Then he signed both of them. That taught me a valuable lesson – never tell another coach what you are thinking. Keep it quiet until they're signed. But we didn't fall out over that – and those two did well for him at Widnes.

I learnt from all the coaches I played for, Vinty Karalius, Frank Myler and Doug. I learnt as well from playing scrum-half for Widnes with Doug at loose-forward. With his guile, he knew what he was doing on the field and in training. He had a great football brain. The Australians wanted people like Doug Laughton, with pace and good handling skills. He could make breaks from nothing, and certainly made me a better player. The opposition were frightened of him, both for what he could do with the ball and that he could look after himself in a scrap.

One special memory of my time playing with Doug was when we played Featherstone in the Challenge Cup semi-final in 1976. Featherstone did a move around the scrum. The scrum-half went on the blind side, left the ball for the loose-forward who would pick it up and put the centre, Newlove, in to score. We had prepared for this in training, but I fell for it, followed the scrum-half and they scored. Doug went mad: "You stupid little b...." he said to me. Fortunately, we fought back and beat then to get to Wembley.

I had some great times with Doug, especially all the Wembley finals and other big matches we played in. But we are friends as well – our families went on holiday together, and there is a camaraderie and mutual respect there. Doug is one of the most respected figures in the game, both here and in Australia. You have to earn that respect. He always wanted to win, he'd give everything in the game. He would say: We're only as strong as our weakest link. Who's that going to be?" He was always the strongest.'

Francis Cummins

'I owe a lot to Doug because he brought me through and as a talent spotter he's second to none, his man management is the best I've ever experienced. He was definitely a player's coach, he did a lot for the players and did a lot for Leeds.

He always had a lot of time for the young players, at the time he turned the club around, he brought a lot of youngsters to the club and a lot of us came through together. He always had time for you, he was always there for you, his office was right next to the changing room, he was always in there and I spent a lot of time with him.

It's the little things that count a lot really to be honest. Sometimes it's more the things that aren't said rather than those that are. I remember the way he was before my first Wembley, he just told me to make sure I go out there and enjoy myself and finished off by saying: 'Don't worry, you'll be playing next week'. He had a lot of time for me, I was just breaking into the side then but it was a quick progression. I can't speak highly enough of him really.

In the dressing room he would basically say to us: 'Time to earn your money now boys, off you go'. I know sometimes things got his back up a bit but he was one of those coaches you know.

He was a star himself, definitely a strong character, very opinionated and wasn't shy about letting you know what his opinion was. He is a terrific character and there are stories involving him still doing the rounds at Leeds after the best part of 10 years.'

Doug Laughton: Statistics and Records

St. Helens
Signed: 1962
Debut: 16 November 1963 vs Featherstone Rovers (H), League, drew 11-11

Wigan
Signed: 16 May 1967, £4,000
Debut: 19 August 1967 vs Salford (H), Lancashire Cup R1, lost 14-18

Widnes
Signed: 6 March 1973, £6,000
Debut: 7 March 1973 vs Salford (H), League, lost 9-18
Last match: 2 September 2 1979 vs Leigh (A), League, lost 22-12

Captained Great Britain in five Test and World Cup matches, including tour
squad to Australia in 1979. In last Great Britain team to win the Ashes 1970
Man of Steel: 1979. Coach of the Year: 1979, 1988
ARL: Played for Canterbury-Bankstown, Australia, 1974

Great Britain test match and World Cup appearances:

1970:

6 June	*Brisbane* vs. Australia	Lost 37-15 (one try)
20 June	*Sydney* vs. Australia	Won 28-7
4 July	*Sydney* vs. Australia	Won 21-17
11 July	*Auckland* vs. New Zealand	Won 19-15 (two tries)
19 July	*Christchurch* vs. New Zealand	Won 23-9 (one try)
World Cup:		
24 October	*Leeds* vs. Australia	Won 11-4
28 October	*Castleford* vs. France	Won 6-0
31 October	*Swinton* vs. New Zealand	Won 27-17 (one try)
7 November	*Leeds* vs. Australia	Lost 7-12

1971:

7 February	*Toulouse* vs. France	Lost 16-8
17 March	*St Helens* vs. France	Won 24-2

1973:

1 December	*Warrington* vs. Australia	Lost 15-5

1974:

20 January	*Grenoble* vs. France	Won 24-5 (one try)
17 February	*Wigan* vs. France	Won 29-0 (one try)

1979:

16 June	*Brisbane* vs. Australia	Lost 35-0

Appearances record

	App.	T	G	Pts	Representative
St. Helens					
1963-64	23	4	0	12	
1964-65	35	5	0	15	Lancs. 2 app, 1t; GB U24 1 app.
1965-66	21	5	0	15	Lancs. 1+1 app, 1t
1966-67	0	0	0	0	
Wigan					
1967-68 ...	32	4	0	12	Lancs. 1+1 app
1968-69 ...	24	4	0	12	
1969-70 ...	49	10	0	30	Lancs. 2 app, 2t
1970-71 ...	39+1	10	0	30	GB 6 app, 1t; Lancs. 2 app, 1t
1971-72 ...	18	4	0	12	
1972-73 ...	21+1	6	0	18	
Widnes					
1972-73 ...	9	3	0	9	
1973-74	25	4	0	12	GB 3 app, 2t; Lancs. 1 app.
1974-75	34	6	0	18	
1975-76	12+1	1	0	3	
1976-77	29+1	3	0	9	England 1 app.
1977-78	37	10	0	30	
1978-79	35+2	9	0	27	
1979-80	1	0	0	0	
Totals					
St. Helens	79	14	0	42	
Wigan	183+2	38	0	114	
Widnes	182+4	36	0	108	
Great Britain	15	7	0	21	
1970 Tour	9	5	0	15	+ 4 tries in 5 Test app.
1979 Tour	4	0	0	0	+ 1 Test app.
England	1	0	0	0	
Great Britain Under-24s	1	0	0	0	
Lancashire	9+2	5	0	15	
GRAND TOTALS	**483+8**	**105**	**0**	**315**	

Cup Final appearances

St. Helens
1963-64 Western Division Final vs. Swinton Won 10-7
1964-65 Championship Final vs. Halifax Lost 15-7
1964-65 Lancashire Cup Final vs. Swinton Won 12-4
1965-66 BBC-2 Floodlit Final vs. Castleford Lost 4-0

Wigan
1968-69 BBC-2 Floodlit Final vs. St Helens Won 7-4
1969-70 RL Challenge Cup Final vs. Castleford Lost 7-2
1969-70 BBC-2 Floodlit Final vs. Leigh Lost 11-6
1970-71 Championship Final vs. St Helens Lost 16-12
1971-72 Lancashire Cup Final vs. Widnes Won 15-8

Widnes
1973-74 BBC-2 Floodlit Final vs. Bramley Lost 15-7
1974-75 RL Challenge Cup Final vs. Warrington Won 14-7
1974-75 Player's No.6 Final vs. Bradford Northern Lost 3-2
1974-75 Lancashire Cup Final vs. Salford Won 6-2
1975-76 RL Challenge Cup Final vs. St Helens Lost 20-5
1976-77 RL Challenge Cup Final vs. Leeds Lost 16-7
1976-77 Lancashire Cup Final vs. Workington Town Won 16-11
1977-78 Premiership Final vs. Bradford Northern Lost 17-8
1977-78 John Player Trophy Final vs. Warrington Lost 9-4
1978-79 RL Challenge Cup Final vs. Wakefield Trinity Won 12-3
1978-79 Lancashire Cup Final vs. Workington Town Won 15-13
1978-79 BBC-2 Floodlit Final vs. St Helens Won 13-7
Member of Widnes 1977-78 Division One championship-winning squad

Summary
RL Challenge Cup Final	Played: 5	Won: 2
Championship Final	Played: 2	Won: 0
Premiership Final	Played: 1	Won: 0
Player's No. 6 Final*	Played: 2	Won: 0
BBC 2 Floodlit Trophy Final	Played: 5	Won: 2
Lancashire Cup Final	Played: 5	Won: 5
Western Division Final	Played: 1	Won: 1
Totals	**Played: 21**	**Won : 10**

Division One championship winners: 1

*The Player's No 6 Trophy became the John Player Trophy and then the Regal Trophy

157

Cup Finals and Charity Shield matches as Coach

Widnes (May 1978 – Mar. 1983; Jan. 1986 – May 1991; Aug. 1995 – May 1997)

1978-79 Lancashire Cup Final vs. Workington Town Won 15-13
1978-79 BBC-2 Floodlit Trophy Final vs. St Helens Won 13-7
1978-79 John Player Trophy Final vs. Warrington Won 28-4
1978-79 RL Challenge Cup Final vs. Wakefield Trinity Won 12-3
1979-80 Lancashire Cup Final vs. Workington Town Won 11-0
1979-80 John Player Trophy Final vs. Bradford Northern Lost 6-0
1979-80 Premiership Final vs. Bradford Northern Won 19-5
1980-81 RL Challenge Cup Final vs. Hull KR Won 18-9
1981-82 Lancashire Cup Final vs. Leigh Lost 8-3
1981-82 RL Challenge Cup Final vs. Hull 14-14 Draw – Lost replay 18-9
1981-82 Premiership Final vs. Hull Won 23-8
1987-88 Premiership Final vs. St Helens Won 38-14
1988-89 Charity Shield vs. Wigan Won 20-14
1988-89 Regal Trophy Final vs. Wigan Lost 12-6
1988-89 Premiership Final vs. Hull Won 18-10
1989-90 Charity Shield vs. Wigan Won 27-22
1989-90 World Club Challenge vs. Canberra Raiders Won 30-18
1989-90 Premiership Final vs. Bradford Northern Won 28-6
1990-91 Charity Shield vs. Wigan Won 24-8
1990-91 Lancashire Cup Final vs. Salford Won 24-18
1990-91 Premiership Final vs. Hull Lost 14-4
Division One champions: 1987-88 and 1988-89

Leeds (May 1991 – Sept. 1995)
1991-92 Regal Trophy Final vs. Widnes Lost 24-0
1993-94 RL Challenge Cup Final vs. Wigan Lost 26-16
1994-95 RL Challenge Cup Final vs. Wigan Lost 30-10
1994-95 Premiership Final vs. Wigan Lost 69-12

Summary

RL Challenge Cup Final	Played: 5	Won: 2
Premiership Final	Played: 7	Won: 5
Regal Trophy Final	Played: 4	Won: 1
BBC 2 Floodlit Trophy Final	Played: 1	Won: 1
Lancashire Cup Final	Played: 4	Won: 3
World Club Challenge	Played: 1	Won: 1
Charity Shield	Played: 3	Won: 3
Total	**Played: 25**	**Won: 16**

Division One championship winners: 2

Lancashire coach: 1981-82, 1988-89, 1989-90: Played: 4 Won 1

Details of Cup Finals and Charity Shield matches

(The details of the Challenge Cup Finals and World Club Challenge are covered in the main text of the book. Doug Laughton's team in bold)

As a player

1963-64 Western Division Final **St. Helens** vs. Swinton Won 10-7
St Helens: Coslett, van Vollenhoven, Williams, Northey, Killeen, Harvey, Murphy, Tembey, Burdell, Owen, French, Warlow, Laughton.
Scorers: Tries: Northey, French. Goals: Coslett (2).
Swinton: Gowers, Speed, Fleet, Parkinson, Stopford, Williams, Cartwright, Bate, Clarke, Halliwell, Morgan, Rees, Blan.
Scorers: Try: Stopford. Goals: Blan (2).

1964-65 Championship Final **St. Helens** vs. Halifax Lost 15-7
St Helens: Barrow, Harvey, van Vollenhoven, Northey, Killeen, Murphy, Smith, Tembey, Dagnall, Watson, French, Mantle, Laughton. Sub: Warlow.
Scorers: Try: Killeen. Goals: Killeen (2).
Halifax: James, Jackson, Burnett, Kellett, Freeman, Robinson, Daley, Roberts, Harrison, Scroby, Fogerty, Dixon, Rennilson.
Scorers: Tries: Burnett (2), Jackson. Goals: James (3).

1964-65 Lancashire Cup Final **St Helens** vs. Swinton Won 12-4
St Helens: Barrow, Pimblett, Northey, Benyon, Killeen, Harvey, Murphy, Tembey, Dagnall, Warlow, French, Hicks, Laughton.
Scorers: Tries: Benyon, Hicks. Goals: Killeen (3).
Swinton: Gowers, Harries, Fleet, Buckley, Speed, Parkinson, Williams, Bate, Clarke, Halliwell, Rees, Simpson, Hurt.
Scorer: Goals: Gowers (2).

1965-66 BBC-2 Floodlit Final **St Helens** vs. Castleford Lost 4-0
St Helens: Barrow, van Vollenhoven, Wood, Benyon, Killeen, Murphy, Prosser, French, Dagnall, Watson, Hicks, Mantle, Laughton.
Castleford: Edwards, C. Battye, M. Battye, Willett, Briggs, Hardisty, Millward, Terry, Ward, Dickinson, Bryant, Small, Taylor.
Scorer: Goals: Willett (2).

1968-69 BBC-2 Floodlit Final **Wigan** vs. St Helens Won 7-4
Wigan: Tyrer, Francis, Ashton, Ashurst, Rowe, Hill, Jackson, Stephens, Clarke, Mills, Fogherty, Kevin O'Loughlin, Laughton. Sub: Lyon.
Scorers: Try: Hill. Goals: Tyrer (2).
St Helens: Williams, Wilson, Benyon, Myler, Wills, Whittle, Bishop, Warlow, Sayer, Watson, Mantle, Hogan, Coslett.
Scorer: Goals: Coslett (2).

1969-70 BBC-2 Floodlit Final **Wigan** vs. Leigh Lost 11-6
Wigan: Hill, Wright, Francis, Rowe, Kevin O'Loughlin, Hill, Jackson, Stephens, Clarke, Ashcroft, Ashurst, Mills, Laughton.
Scorers: Goals: Francis (2), Hill.
Leigh: Ferguson, Tickle, Dorrington, Collins, Walsh, Eckersley, Murphy, Chisnall, Ashcroft, Watts, Welding, Grimes, Lyon. Sub: Lewis.
Scorers: Try: Tickle. Goals: Ferguson (3), Murphy.

1970-71 Championship Final **Wigan** vs. St Helens Lost 16-12
Wigan: Tyrer, Kevin O'Loughlin, Francis, Rower, Wright, Hill, Ayres, Hogan, Clarke, Fletcher, Ashurst, Robinson, Laughton. Sub: Cunningham.
Scorers: Tries: Ashurst, Robinson. Goals: Ashurst (2), Tyrer.
St Helens: Pimblett, Jones, Benyon, Walsh, Blackwood, Whittle, Heaton, Stephens, Karalius, Rees, Mantle, Chisnall, Coslett. Subs: Wanbon, Kelly.
Scorers: Tries: Benyon, Blackwood. Goals: Coslett (5).

1971-72 Lancashire Cup Final **Wigan** vs. Widnes Won 15-8
Wigan: Tyrer, Eastham, Francis, Fuller, Wright, Hill, Ayres, Ashcroft, Clarke, Fletcher, Ashurst, Kevin O'Loughlin, Laughton. Sub: Gandy.
Scorers: Tries: Eastham, Francis, Ayres. Goals: Tyrer.
Widnes: Dutton, Brown, Loughlin, Aspey, Gaydon, O'Neill, Bowden, Warlow, Foran, Doughty, Kirwan, Walsh, Nicholls. Sub: Lowe.
Scorers: Tries: Gaydon, O'Neill. Goal: Aspey.

1973-74 BBC-2 Floodlit Final **Widnes** vs. Bramley Lost 15-7
Widnes: Dutton, O'Neill, Hughes, Aspey, Macko, Warburton, Bowden, Hogan, Elwell, Nelson, Sheridan, Blackwood, Laughton. Sub: Foran.
Scorers: Try: Macko. Goals: Dutton (2).
Bramley: Keegan, Goodchild, Bollon, Hughes, Austin, T. Briggs, Ward, D. Briggs, Firth, Cheshire, Sampson, Idle, Wolford. Sub: Ashman.
Scorers: Tries: Goodchild, Austin, Sampson. Goal: Ward.

1974-75 Player's No.6 Final **Widnes** vs. Bradford Northern Lost 3-2
Widnes: Dutton, Prescott, O'Neill, Aspey, Anderson, Hughes, Bowden, Mills, Elwell, Sheridan, Adams, Blackwood, Laughton.
Scorer: Goal: Dutton.
Bradford Northern: Carlton, Francis, Ward, Gant, Redfearn, Blacker, Seabourne, Earl, Jarvis, Jackson, Joyce, Trotter, Fearnley.
Scorer: Try: Carlton.

1974-75 Lancashire Cup Final **Widnes** vs. Salford Won 6-2
Widnes: Dutton, George, O'Neill, Aspey, Prescott, Hughes, Bowden, Mills, Elwell, Stephens, Adams, Blackwood, Laughton.
Scorers: Try: George. Goal: Dutton. Drop-goal: Hughes.
Salford: Charlton, Fielding, Dixon, Graham, Richards, Taylor, Banner, Mackay, Devlin, Grice, Knighton, Coulman, Prescott.
Scorers: Goal: Fielding.

160

1976-77 Lancashire Cup Final **Widnes** vs. Workington Town Won 16-11
Widnes: Dutton, S. Wright, Aspey, George, Prescott, Eckersley, Bowden, Ramsey, Elwell, Nelson, Dearden, Adams, Laughton.
Scorers: Tries: Wright, George. Goals: Dutton (4). Drop-goals: Dutton, Bowden.
Workington Town: Charlton, Collister, Wilkins, I. Wright, MacCorquodale, Lauder, Walker, Mills, Banks, Calvon, Bowman, L. Gorley, Pattinson. Sub: P. Gorley.
Scorers: Try: Wilkins. Goals: MacCorquodale (4).

1977-78 Premiership Final **Widnes** vs. Bradford Northern Lost 17-8
Widnes: Eckersley, Wright, Hughes, Aspey, Woods, Gill, Bowden, Mills, Elwell, Shaw, Adams, Hull, Laughton. Subs: Ramsey, George.
Scorers: Tries: Aspey (2). Goal: Woods.
Bradford Northern: Mumby, Barends, Roe, Austin, Wolford, Redfearn, I. van Bellen, Raistrick, Thompson, Joyce, Trotter, Haigh. Subs: N. Fox, Forsyth.
Scorers: Tries: Barends, Roe, Redfearn, Haigh. Goals: Mumby (2). Drop-goal: Wolford.

1977-78 John Player Trophy Final **Widnes** vs. Warrington Lost 9-4
Widnes: Eckersley, Wright, Aspey, George, Woods, Hughes, Bowden, Ramsey, Elwell, Shaw, Adams, Hull, Laughton. Sub: Dearden.
Scorer: Goals: Woods (2).
Warrington: Finningan, Hesford, Benyon, F. Wilson, J. Wilson, Kelly, Gordon, Lester, Dalgreen, Nicholas, Martyn, Philbin, Potter.
Scorers: Try: J. Wilson. Goals: Hesford (3).

1978-79 Lancashire Cup Final **Widnes** vs. Workington Town Won 15-13
Widnes: Eckersley, Wright, Aspey, George, Burke, Hughes, Bowden, Mills, Elwell, Shaw, Adams, Dearden, Laughton. Subs: Hull, Woods.
Scorers: Tries: Laughton (2), Wright. Goals: Burke (3).
Workington Town: Charlton, Collister, Risman, Wilkins, MacCorquodale, McMillan, Walker, Beverley, Banks, Bowman, P.Gorley, Blackwood, Pattinson. Sub: L. Gorley.
Scorers: Tries: Wilkins, MacCorquodale, L. Gorley. Goals: MacCorquodale (2).

1978-79 BBC-2 Floodlit Final **Widnes** vs. St Helens Won 13-7
Widnes: Eckersley, Wright, Hughes, Aspey, P. Shaw, Burke, Bowden, Hogan, Elwell, Mills, Adams, Dearden, Laughton.
Scorers: Tries: Wright (2), Burke. Goals: Burke (2).
St Helens: Pimblett, Jones, Glynn, Cunningham, Mathias, Francis, Holding, D. Chisnall, Liptrot, James, Nicholls, Knighton, Pinner. Sub: E. Chisnall.
Scorers: Try: D. Chisnall. Goals: Pimblett (2).

Widnes 1977-78 Division One championship-winning squad
Played: 30. Won: 24. Draw: 2. Lost: 4. Points: 50.
Points scored for: 613. Points conceded: 241.

As a coach
(1978-79 included above in section as a player.)

1979-80 Lancashire Cup Final **Widnes** vs. Workington Town Won 11-0
Widnes: Eckersley, Wright, Aspey, Hughes, Burke, Moran, Bowden, Hogan, Elwell, Shaw, L. Gorley, Dearden, Adams. Subs: George, Hull.
Scorers: Tries: Moran, Adams. Goals: Burke (2). Drop-goal: Elwell.
Workington Town: Charlton, MacCorquodale, Maughan, Thompson, Beck, Rudd, Walker, Beverley, Banks, Wallbanks, Pattinson, Lewis, Dobie. Subs: Roper, Varty.

1979-80 John Player Trophy Final **Widnes** vs. Bradford Northern Lost 6-0
Widnes: Eckersley, Wright, Aspey, George, Burke, Hughes, Bowden, Hogan, Elwell, Shaw, L. Gorley, Hull, Adams. Subs: Mills, Dearden.
Bradford Northern: Mumby, Barends, D. Redfearn, Parker, Gant, Stephenson, A. Redfearn, Thompson, Bridges, Forsyth, Grayshon, G. van Bellen, Casey. Subs: Ferres, I. van Bellen.
Scorers: Try: Parker. Goal: Mumby. Drop-goal: Stephenson.

1979-80 Premiership Final **Widnes** vs. Bradford Northern Won 19-5
Widnes: Burke, Wright, George, Aspey, Bentley, Eckersley, Bowden, Shaw, Elwell, O'Neill, L. Gorley, Hull, Adams. Subs: Moran, Hogan.
Scorers: Tries: Wright, Aspey, Bentley, Elwell, Gorley. Goal: Burke. Drop-goals: Eckersley, Elwell.
Bradford Northern: Mumby, MacLean, D. Redfearn, Parker, Gant, Stephenson, A. Redfearn, Thompson, Bridges, Forsyth, Clarkson, Grayshon, Hale. Subs: Ferres, G. van Bellen.
Scorers: Try: MacLean. Goal: Mumby.

1981-82 Lancashire Cup Final **Widnes** vs. Leigh Lost 8-3
Widnes: Burke, George, Hughes, Cunningham, Bentley, Moran, Gregory, M. O'Neill, Elwell, Lockwood, L. Gorley, E. Prescott, Adams.
Scorers: Try: Bentley.
Leigh: Hogan, Drummond, Bilsbury, Donlan, Worgan, Woods, Green, Wilkinson, Tabern, Cooke, Martyn, Clarkson, McTigue. Sub: B. Platt
Scorers: Try: Bilsbury. Goals: Woods (2). Drop-goal: Donlan.

1981-82 Premiership Final **Widnes** vs. Hull Won 23-8
Widnes: Burke, S. Wright, Keiron O'Loughlin, Cunningham, Basnett, Hughes, Gregory, M. O'Neill, Elwell, Lockwood, L. Gorley, Prescott, Adams. Subs: A. Myler, Whitfield.
Scorers: Tries: Burke, Wright, Basnett, Hughes, Adams. Goals: Burke (4)
Hull: Kemble, O'Hara, Leuluai, S. Evans, Prendiville, Topliss, Harkin, Tindall, Wileman, Stone, Skerrett, L. Crooks, Norton. Subs: Day, Lloyd.
Scorers: Try: Crooks. Goals: Crooks (2). Drop-goal: Crooks.

1987-88 Premiership Final **Widnes** vs. St Helens Won 38-14
Widnes: Platt, Thackray, Currier, D. Wright, Offiah, Dowd, D. Hulme, Sorensen, McKenzie, Grima, M. O'Neill, P. Hulme, R. Eyres. Subs: Tait, S. O'Neill.
Scorers: Tries: Wright (2), D. Hulme (2), Tait, Sorensen, McKenzie. Goals: Currier (4), Platt.
St Helens: Loughlin, Ledger, Tanner, Elia, Quirk, Bailey, Holding, Burke, Groves, Evans, Forber, Fieldhouse, Haggerty. Subs: Dwyer, Allen.
Scorers: Tries: Ledger, Haggerty. Goals: Loughlin (3).

1988-89 Charity Shield **Widnes** vs. Wigan Won 20-14
Widnes: Tait, Thackray, Currier, D. Wright, Offiah, Dowd, D. Hulme, Sorensen, McKenzie, Grima, M. O'Neill, P. Hulme, Eyres. Subs: S. O'Neill, Pyke.
Scorers: Tries: Offiah, Wright, McKenzie. Goals: Currier (4).
Wigan: Hampson, Gill, Lydon, Bell, Preston, Byrne, Gregory, Shelford, Kiss, Case, T. Iro, Wane, Goodway. Subs: Betts, Lucas.
Scorers: Tries: Iro (2), Lydon. Goal: Lydon.

1988-89 John Player Trophy Final **Widnes** vs. Wigan Lost 12-6
Widnes: Tait, Thackray, Currier, D. Wright, Offiah, A. Myler, D. Hulme, Sorensen, McKenzie, Grima, M. O'Neill, Koloto. Subs: P. Hulme, Dowd.
Scorers: Try: Wright, Goal: Currier.
Wigan: Hampson, Bell, K. Iro, Lydon, T. Iro, Byrne, Edwards, Shelford, Dermott, Wane, Betts, Potter, Hanley. Subs: Gregory, Goodway.
Scorers: Tries: K. Iro, Hanley. Goals: Lydon (2).

1988-89 Premiership Final **Widnes** vs. Hull Won 18-10
Widnes: Tait, Davies, Currier, D. Wright, Offiah, D. Hulme, P. Hulme, Sorensen, McKenzie, Grima, M. O'Neill, Koloto, R. Eyres. Subs: Pyke, A. Myler.
Scorers: Tries: Currier, Wright, Offiah. Goals: Davies (3).
Hull: Fletcher, Eastwood, Blacker, Price, O'Hara, Pearce, Windley, Dannatt, L. Jackson, S. Crooks, Welham, Sharp, Divorty. Subs: Wilby, R. Nolan.
Scorers: Try: Welham. Goals: Pearce (3).

1989-90 Charity Shield **Widnes** vs. Wigan Won 27-22
Widnes: Tait, Kebbie, Davies, D. Wright, Offiah, A. Myler, D. Hulme, Sorensen, P. Hulme, Grima, M. O'Neill, Koloto, Eyres. Subs: Marsh, Pyke.
Scorers: Tries: Kebbie, Offiah, Davies. Goals: Davies (5). Drop-goal: Tait.
Wigan: Hampson, Bell, K. Iro, Lydon, Preston, Byrne, Gregory, Lucas, Kiss, Platt, Betts, Gildart, Goodway. Subs: Gilfillan, Stazicker.
Scorers: Tries: Platt, Lydon, Iro. Goals: Lydon (5).

1989-90 Premiership Final **Widnes** vs. Bradford Northern Won 28-6
Widnes: Tait, Davies, Currier, D. Wright, Offiah, D. Hulme, P. Hulme, Sorensen, McKenzie, M. O'Neill, Koloto, R. Eyres, Holliday. Subs: A. Myler, Grima.
Scorers: Tries: Tait (2), Currier (2), Holliday. Goals: Davies (4).
Bradford N: Wilkinson, Cordle, McGowan, Marchant, Francis, Simpson, Harkin, Skerrett, Noble, Hobbs, Medley, Fairbank, Mumby. Subs: Cooper, Richards.
Scorers: Try: Marchant. Goal: Mumby.

1990-91 Charity Shield **Widnes** vs. Wigan Won 24-8
Widnes: Tait, Devereux, Currier, Davies, Offiah, A. Myler, D. Hulme, Ashurst, McKenzie, Grima, P. Hulme, Koloto, Holliday. Subs: D. Wright, Sorensen.
Scorers: Tries: Davies (3), Devereux, Offiah. Goals: Davies (2).
Wigan: Gilfillan, Myers, Bell, Byrne, Preston, Botica, Goulding, Skerrett, Bridge, Wane, Gildart, Platt, Betts. Subs: Edwards, Forshaw.
Scorers: Try: Botica. Goals: Botica (2).

1990-91 Lancashire Cup Final **Widnes** vs. Salford Won 24-18
Widnes: Tait, D. Wright, Currier, Davies, Offiah, A. Myler, D. Hulme, Sorensen, McKenzie, Ashurst, Eyres, Koloto, Holliday. Subs: Devereux, D. Smith.
Scorers: Tries: Currier, Myler, Smith, Offiah. Goals: Davies (4).
Salford: Gibson, Evans, Birkett, Williams, Hadley, Fell, Kerry, Sherratt, Lee, Whiteley, Bradshaw, Blease, Burgess. Subs: Cassidy, Hansen.
Scorers: Tries: Williams, Blease, Fell. Goals: Kerry (3).

1990-91 Premiership Final **Widnes** vs. Hull Lost 14-4
Widnes: Tait, Devereux, Currier, Davies, Offiah, Dowd, D. Hulme, Sorensen, McKenzie, Grima, P. Hulme, Koloto, McCurrie. Subs: Howard, D. Wright.
Scorer: Try: Offiah.
Hull: Gay, Eastwood, McGarry, Webb, Turner, Mackey, Entat, Harrison, L. Jackson, Dannatt, Marlow, Walker, Sharp. Subs: Busby, G. Nolan.
Scorers: Tries: Eastwood, Walker, G. Nolan. Goal: Eastwood.

Widnes Division One Champions: 1987-88 and 1988-89
1987-88 Played: 26. Won: 20. Draw: 0. Lost: 6. Points: 40.
Points scored for: 641. Points conceded: 311.
1988-89 Played: 26. Won: 20. Draw: 1. Lost: 5. Points: 41.
Points scored for: 726. Points conceded: 345.

1991-92 Regal Trophy Final **Leeds** vs. Widnes Lost 24-0
Leeds: Edwards, Ford, Creasser, Irving, Bentley, Schofield, Goulding, Wane, Gunn, O'Neill, Powell, Dixon, Divorty. Subs: Gibson, Molloy.
Widnes: Tait, Devereux, Currier, D. Wright, Sarsfield, Davies, Dowd, Sorensen, P. Hulme, D. Smith, Howard, R. Eyres, Holliday. Subs: Atcheson, Grima.
Scorers: Tries: Tait, Davies, Sorensen, Holliday. Goals: Davies (3). Drop-goals: Davies, Holliday.

1994-95 Premiership Final **Leeds** vs. Wigan Lost 69-12
Leeds: Tait, Fallon, Iro, Hassan, Cummins, Innes, Holroyd, Howard, Lowes, Faimalo, Mann, Eyres, Mercer. Subs: Vassilakopoulos, Harmon.
Scorers: Tries: Innes, Eyres. Goals: Holroyd (2).
Wigan: Paul, Robinson, Radlinski, Connolly, Offiah, Botica, Edwards, Skerrett, Hall, Cowie, Betts, Farrell, Clarke. Subs: Cassidy, Haughton.
Scorers: Tries: Radlinski (3), Connolly (3), Paul, Edwards, Skerrett, Hall, Betts, Haughton. Goals: Botica (10). Drop-goal: Farrell.

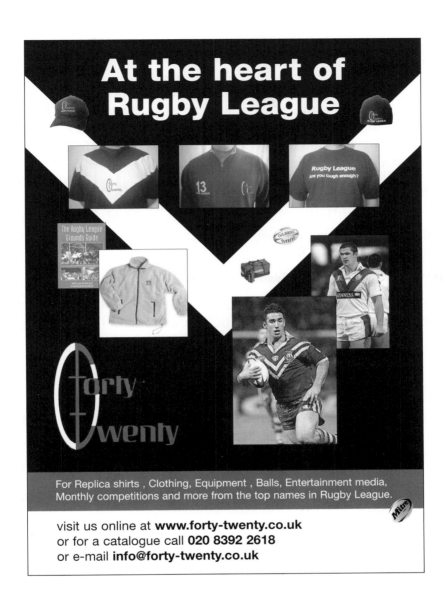

Kevin Sinfield: Life with Leeds Rhinos
A 2003 Rugby League Diary
By Kevin Sinfield with Philip Gordos

Kevin Sinfield's diary of the dramatic 2003 Leeds Rhinos season will be of interest to all Rugby League followers.

In his first season as captain, he lifts the lid on life on and off the pitch at Headingley.

The book gives Kevin's inside story on:

- Leeds Challenge Cup campaign, including the nail-biting semi-final victory over St Helens, and the bitter final defeat to the Bradford Bulls;
- The roller-coaster battle for the Super League Crown;
- The players' reaction to the imprisonment of two of their team mates and the shock decision of Daryl Powell to step down as coach;
- The club's fitness and training regimes;
- The responsibilities of being captain at just 22

The book is well illustrated throughout with photos by local photographer David Williams

All Rugby League followers will enjoy this book.

About the author: In May 1997, an article in *Open Rugby* described Kevin Sinfield as 'the best schoolboy player ever seen'. Hardly surprising then, that Leeds, whom he joined after leaving school, handed him his first-team debut at the age of just 16. Six years later, Kevin is now captain of the Rhinos and an established international, having represented England in the 2000 World Cup and played for Great Britain against Australia and New Zealand in 2001 and 2002. A model professional, Kevin is a member of David Waite's initial 30-man squad for November's Ashes Series against the Kangaroos.

To be published in November 2003 at £9.95. Special offer for readers of this boo: £9.00 post free. ISBN: 1903659-13-2. Order from: London League Publications, PO Box 10441, London E14 0SB. Cheques only, credit cards via our website: www.llpshop.co.uk

Published twice a year at £2.50

The magazine for Rugby League supporters who want an in-depth analysis of the game.

Four issue subscription: £9.00 (cover price £2.50).
Back numbers available: 1 to 7: £1.50 each or £7 for all 7.
Special £12 offer:
Three issue subscription plus a copy of **one** of the following books:
- *Tries in the Valleys – A History of Rugby League in Wales*
- *From Fulham to Wembley – 20 years of Rugby League in London*
- *The Fulham Dream – Rugby League comes to London*
- *Rugby League Bravehearts – A history of Scottish Rugby League*

SUBSCRIPTION FORM

I would like the following subscription: (tick box)
4 issues - £9.00   []
3 issues plus a book £12.00   []

Subscription to start with issue no.:
Book chosen (3 issue sub):
Back numbers at £1.50 each:
Full set of back numbers - £7:   []

Name:

Address:

Telephone: Email:

Please send to: London League Publications Ltd, Po Box 10441, London E14 0SB. Cheques payable to London League Publications Ltd. Credit card orders via our website: www.llpshop.co.uk. **Photocopy** if you do not want to cut the book, or provide these details when you order.

167

Books about three great players:

The Great Bev - The rugby league career of Brian Bevan
By Robert Gate

Brian Bevan is one of the few rugby league players to rightfully be called a Legend. He scored 796 tries in British rugby league, a record that will never be surpassed. He had remarkable fitness, pace, side-step and anticipation for try scoring. The book covers his early days in Australian rugby league, his war-time experiences, joining Warrington and his triumphs there, including the 1950 and 1954 Challenge Cup victories. Also included are his international appearances with the Other Nationalities team, his time with Blackpool at the end of his career, and memories of him from fellow players and supporters. Lavishly illustrated, the book also has a comprehensive statistical record of Bevan's career. **Published in August 2002 at £14.95, post free. ISBN: 1-903659-06-X**

I, George Nepia - The Autobiography of a Rugby Legend
By George Nepia and Terry McLean
Foreword by Oma Nepia - New edition with new material

George Nepia is arguably New Zealand's greatest ever Rugby Union player, and someone for whom the word "Legend" is appropriate. At the age of 19, he played every game at full-back for the 1924-5 'Invincibles' tour of England, Wales, Ireland and France, a staggering achievement for one so young. The book recalls a "Golden Age" of Rugby Union in the 1920s and 1930s. First published in 1963, his autobiography covered his early years, the 1924-25 tour; and his Rugby career. This edition has new material that gives a full picture of Nepia's life and rugby career,. including a new chapter by his original collaborator, Terry McLean. There is also a full record of Nepia's time in Rugby League, including for Streatham & Mitcham, Halifax and Manukau. **Published in September 2002 at £13.95. ISBN: 1903659-07-8. Special offer for readers of this book: £10.00 post free.**

Kiwis, Wigan and The Wire - My Life and Rugby League
By Ces Mountford

Ces Mountford is recognised as one of the greatest Kiwi Rugby League players of all time. He joined Wigan in 1946, and was a key member of the great post-war Wigan team. In 1951, he was the first foreign player to win the Lance Todd Trophy. In 1951, he joined Warrington as manager and stayed with the club for 10 years, including some of their greatest triumphs, including the 1954 Cup and Championship Double. He then returned to New Zealand, and developed Rugby League coaching, including managing the national team. **Published in May 2003 at £9.95, post free. ISBN: 1903659-10-8**

All 3 books for £30. Order from: London League Publications, PO Box 10441, London E14 0SB. Cheques to London League Publications Ltd.

Give it to Kelly!
A Rugby League Saga

By John D. Vose

Foreword by John Etty

John D. Vose's new book completes a trilogy about Bramfield Rovers, a fictional struggling Lancashire Rugby League side from the 1930s.

Following on from his previous books *Up t' Rovers* and *Put Ref. A Jersey On!*, this book recalls a more innocent time for the game, away from the modern day pressures of professional sport.

Readers will be entertained and bemused by:

- Club scout Stanley Keighley's scouting mission to a posh North Yorkshire Rugby Union club;
- A wizard centre with a double-barrelled name;
- A Russian spy masquerading as a belly dancer from Heckmondwike on the run from Captain Montague-Morency of MI6; and
- A light-fingered, smooth-talking Australian: a try-scoring rugby genius who can streak past defenders with the agility of a cheetah, beguile Lancashire barmaids and daughters of the aristocracy with equal aplomb, and then set the police forces of Yorkshire and Lancashire hot on his trail.

About the author: John D. Vose grew up in St Helens in the 1930s. He has written widely on many subjects as well as Rugby League. He now lives in Blackpool.

Published in September 2003 at £8.95. Special Offer for readers of this book £8.00 post free. ISBN: 1903659-11-6

Order from: London League Publications Ltd, PO Box 10441, London E14 0SB. Cheques payable to London League Publications Ltd. Credit card orders through our website: www.llpshop.co.uk